Freire and Critical Theorists

FREIRE IN FOCUS

Series editors: Greg William Misiaszek and Carlos Alberto Torres

This series consists of short-format books that provide readers a diverse range of Paulo Freire's work and Freireans' reinventions towards social justice both inside and outside education, without readers needing any prior knowledge of his scholarship. Freire's teaching, ideas, methods, and philosophies. Each book will introduce Freire's work so it is easily understood by a wider audience without overly simplifying the depth of his scholarship.

Freire and Critical Theorists

CRYSTAL GREEN

BLOOMSBURY ACADEMIC
LONDON • NEW YORK • OXFORD • NEW DELHI • SYDNEY

BLOOMSBURY ACADEMIC
Bloomsbury Publishing Plc
50 Bedford Square, London, WC1B 3DP, UK
1385 Broadway, New York, NY 10018, USA
29 Earlsfort Terrace, Dublin 2, Ireland

BLOOMSBURY, BLOOMSBURY ACADEMIC and the Diana logo are
trademarks of Bloomsbury Publishing Plc

First published in Great Britain 2023

Series design by Charlotte James
Cover image © Paulo Freire via Torres, Carlos Alberto (2014). First
Freire: Early writings in social justice education. Teachers College Press.
Background image © ilyast / Getty Images

A catalogue record for this book is available from the British Library.

A catalog record for this book is available from the Library of Congress.

ISBN: HB: 978-1-3503-3370-3
PB: 978-1-3503-3371-0
ePDF: 978-1-3503-3372-7
eBook: 978-1-3503-3373-4

Series: Freire in Focus

Typeset by Deanta Global Publishing Services, Chennai, India

To find out more about our authors and books visit www.bloomsbury.com
and sign up for our newsletters.

CONTENTS

SERIES FOREWORD

Carlos Alberto Torres
  Distinguished Professor,
  Director, Paulo Freire Institute, University of California Los Angeles (UCLA)

The Italian writer Italo Calvino propounded an insightful motto: "A human being becomes human not through the casual convergence of certain biological conditions, but through an act of will and love on the part of other people."[1]

There is no question in my mind that if Paulo Freire would have encountered this motto from Italo Calvino, he would have adopted this sentence for himself. Any discussion of the political anthropology animating Freire's work would have to agree that Freire's emphasis on processes of dehumanization–humanization invites the awareness of such humanizing possibilities, giving rise to a moral obligation that education constitutes a distinctive human "vocation" and one that is infused by love.[2]

Paulo Freire is today one of the educators with the highest international reach in the world.[3] While John Dewey was the best-known Western philosopher of education in the first half of the twentieth century, Freire is today the best-known political philosopher of education in the second half of last century, with much currency in this century.[4]

Just to illustrate this point, let's consider the work of Elliot Green who compiled the most cited publications in the social sciences which shows that *Pedagogy of the Oppressed* ranks third in the twenty-five most cited books in the social sciences (after Thomas Kuhn's *The Structure of the Scientific Revolutions* and Everett Rogers's *Diffusion of Innovations*). In fact, Freire's most famous book, in Green's analysis, is ranked as the most cited book in the field of education.[5]

Following Thomas Kuhn's arguments, one could argue that with the publication of *Pedagogy of the Oppressed*, Freire produced a rapid paradigmatic shift in educational sciences and beyond.

This collection of critical theorists, many of whom informed Freire's theories, will help to fully understand Freire's intellectual roots and theoretical directions. It is a pity that his untimely death in 1997 prevented him from engaging seriously with the theories and epistemologies of some of the writers studied in this volume.

The first scholars discussed in this book, including Erich Fromm, bell hooks, Enrique Dussel, and Franz Fanon, were writers who Freire knew well and in many ways interpellated his theories. Other critical scholars who either preceded Freire like Antonio Gramsci[6] or were his contemporaries like Jürgen Habermas[7] worked on parallel to Freire's work. They have been the object of comparisons about complementarity or convergence in their analyses considering the context of Freire's vision.

Scholars like Nancy Frazer, while not in connection with Freire, discuss issues of identity and redistribution that will be closer to Freire's heart, research agenda, and praxis. Mikael Bakhtin was very influential for Freire and his team in the Secretariat of Public Education in São Paulo, Brazil, when Freire was Secretary of Education (1988–91).[8]

The work of Pierre Bourdieu, arguably the most important sociologist in the second half of the twentieth century; the forceful works of Michel Foucault; and the imaginative, lucid, and rigorous analysis of Iris Young, while not exactly related to Freire's work, open magnificent vistas to compare and contrast with Freire's contributions.

Written by Dr. Crystal Green as an anthology of biographies, concepts, theories, and policy orientations that impacted the social sciences and eventually Freire, each chapter is also an introduction to remarkable thinkers and their *oeuvres*.

Many Freireans have used the prisms of these scholars to inspect diverse facets of Freire's lifeworld, work, and theories. This book will open up new dimensions in the study of Freire and his contributions to education.

ACKNOWLEDGMENTS

This book is the product of my time at the University of California, Los Angeles, as a visiting graduate student and postdoctoral scholar. For that opportunity, I owe a debt of gratitude to Richard Desjardins, whose encouragement, insight, and humor supported my professional development throughout my time at UCLA. It is rare to find a mentor as engaging as Richard, who gives time to his students and to the development of the university so generously. The clarity of his guidance propelled me into a most meaningful and productive season of my own work, and it was Richard who, together with the remarkable Susan Wiksten, encouraged me to seek out Carlos Alberto Torres while at UCLA.

I am grateful to Carlos for many things, among them the invitation to write this book. Carlos is a kind and gracious spirit, with a curiosity and warmth that invites others to learn from and with him. As a student and colleague, I have known Carlos as a storyteller with an incredible memory, able to convey meaning with gravitas, yet quick to lighten the room in the ease of his laughter. I thank Carlos for his attentiveness to his graduate students, and to the graduate students who journeyed together with us through the readings and lectures that became the basis for this book; thank you for your engaged and enthusiastic discussions.

Thank you to the Fulbright Scholar researching in Brazil in 2006, whose name I cannot remember and cannot find. She appears in my memory now as an apparition, walking me through the streets of Buenos Aires to the Ateneo Grand Splendid to introduce me to the work of Paulo Freire. Many thanks to Katariina Tiainen and Greg Misiaszek for detailed comments on earlier drafts of this book, and especially to

Kristiina Brunila for the encouraging comments and for trumpeting not only my work but the work of all your fellow critical feminist scholars. To Weldon, thank you for your indefatigable patience and love. To Emilia, Beth, and John, thank you for caring for the little ones so I could write. To Lisa and Thomas, thank you for your determined commitment to my own literacy and political awareness. And to my Bastian, Alli, Leo, and Raz—may you grow up learning to read the world and the word.

Introduction

*Consistent with the liberating purpose of dialogical
education, the object of the investigation is not
persons (as if they were anatomical fragments),
but rather the thought-language with which men
and women refer to reality, the levels at which they
perceive that reality, and their view of the world, in
which their generative themes are found.*

—PAULO FREIRE

A hundred years ago, Edeltrudis Veves Freire gave birth to
the youngest of her four children, Paulo Regulus, at her home
in Recife, Pernumbuco, Brazil. In the years that followed,
Edeltrudis and her husband Joaquin Temístocles gave Paulo
his first lessons in reading and writing under the shade of the
mango trees in their backyard, teaching him by example the
importance of dialogue and respecting one another's beliefs.
Although Freire's parents were middle class, his childhood
and schooling were shaped by bouts of poverty and hunger—
experiences which led to his conviction that "the world needed
to be corrected" and an abiding sense of hope and optimism
about the possibility for social transformation.[1]

In 2021, as we celebrate the centennial of Paulo Freire's birth
and reflect on his legacy and the continual possibility for social
transformation, it remains important to situate Freire within
the histories that produced his own unique biography. In this
book, which aims to elaborate Freire's work in relation to his

contemporary twentieth-century critical scholars, I interpret Freire's invocation to read the word and the world as a motion toward the historical embeddedness of social theories and the contextuality of our relations with one another. This book is an encounter with Freire alongside his contemporaries, generating a kaleidoscopic view toward their shared and disparate ideas, experiences, and dreams.

To be literate of the twentieth-century requires engagement with the contexts and ideologies of the epochs these intellectuals were shaped by and also the worlds that they transformed. We linger with these selected scholars with the knowledge that their past is unfinished and comprehensible only in part. What these scholars share is a critique of domination, oppression, and state violence. The relevance of Freire, in his time and now, speaks to the organization of modern society and its systemic oppressions.

Like all enduring critical theory, Freire helps us examine social relations and our own experiences, bringing an analytical clarity and a language to describe violence and alienation within an unjust social order. Freire provides a framework for understanding how teachers reproduce oppression through their daily interactions with students, as well as how teachers and students can become conscious of themselves as political actors. His social analysis disrupts hierarchies between students and teachers, emphasizing the humanity of the learner and demystifying methods of (de)humanization in the classroom.

Although Freire remains an international thought leader, there are limits to his influence. After Freire's passing in 1997, Donaldo Macedo gave a pointed critique of the Harvard Graduate School of Education (HGSE) in his foreword to the English translation of *Pedagogy of Freedom*. Macedo described the use of Freire's work in the curriculum of the Harvard Divinity School in the late 1990s but, as Howard Gardner later put it, "excoriates" HGSE, observing that

> the Harvard Graduate School of Education's interest in [Freire's] ideas and work was purely a matter of public

relations. In other words it is acceptable to embrace Freire as an icon for one semester to legitimize the Harvard Graduate School of Education's claim of openness, diversity, and democracy, but it is not acceptable to allow his ideas to become part of the general course offerings. Even though Freire has been considered the most important educator in the last half of this century, the Harvard Graduate School of Education does not offer a single course designed specifically to study Freire's theories and ideas.[2]

A bit more than a decade after Freire's death and the publication of Macedo's commentary, I was a graduate student at HGSE. In my experience, Macedo's critique holds. At the 2013 Askwith Forum celebrating the forty-fifth publication of Freire's seminal *Pedagogy of the Oppressed*, Howard Gardner, Noam Chomsky, and Bruno della Chiesa were invited to discuss Freire's work.[3] When Gardner asked how familiar the audience was with Freire, the majority said they had a superficial knowledge, and only a small handful were intimately familiar with his work and its relation to critical theory. Swati Sahni, a graduate student at HGSE who spoke from the audience, noted "an absolute absence of Freire's name anywhere" in the curriculum and coursework and "no thought around Freire's work." She related this to the wider situation at Harvard, where "there is no space for Marxist thought." I would add here that without dialogue around Marxist thought, there can be no substantial critique of it, only subsidiary commentary. The conversation then turned to why Freire is absent, Bruno della Cheisa commenting, "it's enough for some people in our society to just discard it and say this is dangerous stuff." Howard Gardner clarified that the critique would be not that Freire is dangerous but "equally damning" that "it's irrelevant."

That Freire is largely absent at HGSE is perhaps symptomatic of the wider contemporary problem of dismissing political opposition as unworthy of dialogue. It is perhaps also symptomatic of an entrenching polarization of radical certainties on both the right and the left that, as Freire notes, "suffer from an absence of doubt." Bruno della Cheisa makes the case for the ongoing relevance of a dialogue with the intellectual currents which have galvanized social movements over time, both institutional movements and movements of resistance. Therefore I agree with Howard Gardner's suggestion that Harvard "would do well to be much more alert to intellectual currents, including ones that might make us uncomfortable." This volume is therefore also an invitation to a systematic, nuanced, and dialogical elaboration of those intellectual currents, particularly of critical theory in education, which make some people uncomfortable and propel others to sustained social action.

Freire is iconic yet his ideas are not singular. Central themes of his work such as oppression, love, and praxis are also themes in the work of his contemporaries. In this way, Freire was a social theorist and a humanist, drawing on and reinterpreting the Marxist tradition of critical theory. As a critical theorist, Freire works to explain the social structures of society and the mechanisms, purposes, and functions of oppression. However, this book also follows the notion that Freire cannot be taken *as such* without dialogue, without reinvention. Likewise, each of the scholars selected has made prolific contributions. The readings given in this book are necessarily selective. First, it is selective of those pieces which are most relevant to the themes of Freire's work. Second, there are limitations of space. For educators, this book is a resource—an introduction to a series of conversations with students about questions of social power, justice, the limits and possibilities of education and pedagogy to address injustice, to change practices and structures of oppression, and to resist alienation. For scholars, the book gives indications of the basis for theoretical frameworks which merge Freire with his contemporary social theories. This book is an invitation to reinvent Freire through the works of his contemporaries, to see how Freire himself has reinvented his contemporaries, and to join with Freire in, as Freire put it, "moving out on [one's] own" to understand what it means to be democratic each in our own context.[4]

Method

The choice of the eleven authors selected for this book developed organically from a dialogue between myself and Carlos Alberto Torres during my postdoctoral research at the University of California, Los Angeles. Initially, my interest was in reading writers that influenced Torres's work, in an effort to expand my own fluency with the sociology of education under his mentorship. As we began discussing, we decided that it would be interesting to put these authors in conversation with Freire's work and to develop this conversation into a seminar for his doctoral students. In organizing the lectures, we expanded the selection of critical social theorists to consider also the philosophical influences on my own intellectual development. In the end, we chose those theorists who have both influenced and been influenced by Freire, as well as writers who are working with the generative themes that have been influential for Torres and myself. Following Torres's insight that "if you scratch a theory, you find a biography,"[5] we decided that the lectures would elaborate on not only the intellectual but also the biographical profiles of the selected scholars.

Eleven twentieth-century critical philosophers are chosen for inclusion in this book: Erich Fromm, bell hooks, Enrique Dussel, Frantz Fanon, Antonio Gramsci, Jürgen Habermas, Nancy Fraser, Mikhail Bakhtin, Michel Foucault, Pierre Bourdieu, and Iris Young. The order of the presentation of the authors flows from Freire himself. Fromm and hooks Freire knew personally; Dussel was directly influenced by Freire; Fanon and Gramsci were direct intellectual influences on Freire himself. Then follow the authors whose works have been put into dialogue with Freire by other scholars, first those who have been influential on the work of Torres (Habermas and Fraser) and lastly those who have influenced me (Bakhtin, Foucault, Bourdieu, and Young).

The book takes as a methodological starting point Freire's commitment to dialogue. Dyadic analysis,[6] a research method for connecting themes across and between texts, is used to look at the writings of Freire and each theorist. I present quotations from each author to develop the sense of dialogic encounter between the two writers. By curating each pairing of Freire with another (the "dyad") a third voice emerges in the analysis, which is my own. Dyadic analysis is a reciprocal process of looking back and forth between the authors in a process of reading them together. This analysis is supplemented with contextual and biographical material from scholarship dedicated to interpreting the lives and works of each scholar, and existing scholarship on connections between each theorist and Freire. The aim is not a Freirean critique of each author nor the application of other critical theories to critique Freire. Rather, each chapter works at drawing out meaningful links and disjunctures between the themes relevant to their works and to the ongoing development of critical theory and the reinvention of Freire's work. The analytical perspective therefore investigates what Freire has called the *thematic universes* or *meaningful thematics* of these twentieth-century scholars, looking for the synergies, shared realities which shaped Freire and his contemporaries. This follows Freire's commitment to a dialogic method, "affording the opportunity both to discover generative themes and to stimulate people's awareness in regard to these themes" in an effort to understand each theme "in its richness, its significance, its plurality, its transformations, and its historical composition."[7]

Each chapter presents a brief biography that aims to reflect on the conditions which formed each of these scholars, the worlds that meditated them and to which they spoke. Biographies are highlighted with the intent to demythologize these intellectuals, to draw attention to their dynamism, and to contextualize each scholar with their thoughts in order to consider more deeply the significance of the themes they raise. According to Freire, "themes exist within people."[8] The book therefore takes a biographical and historiographical approach to the authors in their cultural contexts, maintaining a focus on the themes which emerge from their particular realities, rather than on the mythos of the authors themselves. Antagonisms and analogies are woven through the book, pointing to directions for further dialogue.

Outline of Chapters

The first four chapters present theorists closest to Freire in terms of direct personal and intellectual connections. Chapter 1 presents Erich Fromm, elaborating themes of necrophilia and biophilia, freedom and alienation, drawing connections to *Pedagogy of the Oppressed*. Chapter 2 presents Gloria Watkins, pen name bell hooks, who was directly influenced by Freire as student and comrade. Themes of pedagogy, Black subjectivity, love, and praxis are presented in this chapter. Drawing on hooks's critique, questions of race and feminism in Freire's work are raised. Enrique Dussel is introduced in Chapter 3. Dussel's perspectives on the philosophy of liberation are discussed, including themes of Otherness and the poor, the Global South, oppression and dependency. Shared perspectives are presented on Marx and materiality, praxis and ethics, as well as Dussel's elaboration of dialectics and analectics. Frantz Fanon is presented in Chapter 4, focusing on themes of Black consciousness, language, colonization, and liberation. A critical discussion is developed on the question of violence in Freire's work and the impact of Freire's time in Africa on his perspective on colonization and liberation. Chapter 5 introduces Antonio Gramsci, drawing parallels to Freire's experience as a political prisoner and orientation toward the Humanist Marxist tradition. The chapter draws on the work of Peter Mayo to address Freire and Gramsci's explicit concern for education, as well as critiques of their use of dichotomous oppositions to analyze social relations.

Chapter 6 presents Jurgen Habermas, and themes of communicative action, deliberative democracy, and critical emancipatory knowledge are elaborated. The work of Raymond Allen Morrow and Carlos Alberto Torres[9] is used to elaborate the connection between Habermas and Freire, including their interest in humanism, the relationship between the social and the onto-epistemic through human communication. The importance of language and linguistics, the separation of the cognitive from the social, and identity in Freire's work are discussed. Nancy Fraser's themes of justice, (mis)recognition, participatory parity, and dialogue are outlined in Chapter 7, and a discussion introduced of Freire's treatment of race and gender in relation to justice as a legal and dialogic accomplishment.

Mikael Bakhtin's biography is introduced in Chapter 8, highlighting his political exile and experience as an amputee. Themes of dialogue and discourse, carnival, and the unfinalized are described, connecting and contrasting Bakhtin's interest in the fantastic, the idea of "double-voiced discourse," and how we emerge as dialogical and relational beings in the world. Chapter 9 gives a brief introduction to Michel Foucault and his methods, including Foucauldian discourse analysis and genealogical methods. Power, biopower/biopolitics, bodies, subjectification, and domination are described, raising questions about Freire's treatment of the body as a site of domination and liberation, and the relation between Foucault's ideas of technique and Freire's conceptualization of pedagogy. Chapter 10 emphasizes Pierre Bourdieu's interest in the sociology of culture and the reproduction of power, especially in educational settings. Themes of social capital, symbolic violence, habitus, cultural reproduction, and doxa are introduced, drawing connections with the role of the teachers in maintaining the dominant culture and the need for critical sociology of education which analyzes both the macro (structural) and the micro (pedagogical). Chapter 11 presents

Iris Young, focusing on themes of oppression, justice, and difference. Young's description of oppression is discussed at length, with connections to Freire's descriptions of oppression. In the final chapter, "Unfinished Conversations," I reflect on the process of writing the book, outlining possible avenues for future research agendas. I provide a concluding synthesis and an invitation to further dialogue.

CHAPTER 1

Freire and Fromm

Erich Fromm was perhaps one of the most influential thinkers on Paulo Freire's writing, and Freire's work was cited by Fromm as well.[1] Freire and Fromm were not only contemporaries but knew each other personally. In the late 1960s, Freire visited Fromm on more than one occasion in Cuernavaca, Mexico. These meetings were arranged by Ivan Illich, author of *Deschooling Society* (1971), through Illich's Centro Intercultural de Documentación (CIDOC),[2] which operated for the "emancipation of politically-oppressed Latin Americans."[3]

Rosa Krause Fromm gave birth to Erich Fromm in 1900 in Frankfurt, Germany. Erich was the only child of Rosa and her husband Naphtali Fromm. Erich later described his mother as narcissistic, depressive, and possessive, traits which manifest in his close relationship with her and in tensions between his mother and father. Fromm described his upbringing in the tradition of Orthodox Judaism, saying that his "spiritual home" had a "medieval atmosphere." In this environment, he was taught to value learning and wisdom, and to seek spiritual maturity through studying the Talmud with his great-uncle. Fromm's biographer Rainer Funk notes this upbringing as being quite different from the "bourgeois-liberal spirit of Frankfurt at the beginning of the twentieth century," which Fromm found strange and preoccupied with money. Fromm's traditional upbringing "spurred [him] on to self-confidence and the discovery of his own identity." Fromm earned a doctorate in sociology from the University of Heidelberg at the age of twenty-two and went on to be trained in psychoanalysis.

In approaching questions of society and human freedom from a psychoanalytic perspective, Fromm made a point of distinguishing himself from certain social theorists, who came before him. In *Escape from Freedom*, Fromm writes that his book "disagrees . . . emphatically with those theories which neglect the role of the human factor as one of the dynamic elements in the social process."[4] Fromm goes on,

> This criticism is directed not only against sociological theories which explicitly wish to eliminate psychological problems from sociology (like those of Durkheim and his school), but also against those theories that are more or less tinged with behaviouristic psychology. Common to all these theories is the assumption that human nature has no dynamism of its own and that psychological changes are to be understood in terms of the development of new "habits" as an adaptation to new cultural patterns. These theories, though speaking of the psychological factor, at the same time reduce it to a shadow of cultural patterns.

Drawing on both Marx and Freud, Fromm wanted to understand humanity from a perspective which is both psychological and social, and in which the psychological is specifically influenced by the social. Fromm was interested in the economic and cultural roots of personality, and the idea that personality is to a considerable extent a reflection of social class, minority status, education, vocation, religious and philosophical background, and so forth.

Like other Jewish philosophers of the Frankfurt school who came to the United States as the Nazis rose to power in the 1930s, Fromm was interested in understanding how and why people came to tolerate their own oppression under fascism, to submit to authority and external control. Fromm's first book *Fear of Freedom*, alternately translated *Escape from Freedom*, was published several years into the Second World War. Fromm begins the book with a reflection about a shared sense during the interwar period that there was a clear move toward liberalism, democracy, and expanding rights.

> The World War was regarded by many as the final struggle and its conclusion the ultimate victory for freedom. Existing democracies appeared strengthened, and new ones replaced old monarchies. But only a few years elapsed before new systems emerged which denied everything that men believed they had won in centuries of struggle. For the essence of these new systems, which effectively took command of man's entire social and personal life, was the submission of all but a handful of men to an authority over which they had no control.

As a humanistic philosopher, Fromm was interested in the question of freedom, but also its opposite: violence and totalitarianism. Fromm approaches these questions from the psychoanalytic school of critical theory, which is concerned with themes of alienation and domination, in terms of making a diagnosis of humanity. "If we want to fight Fascism we must understand it," Fromm says.[5]

In *The Heart of Man*, from which Freire quotes in *Pedagogy of the Oppressed*, Fromm approaches the question of humanity from the psychoanalytic perspective of syndromes, distinguishing between two syndromes: the syndrome of decay and the syndrome of growth. Fromm first distinguishes between forms of violence. Yet beyond this violence, Fromm says, there is something darker, which is even unlike Freud's idea of a primal or ancient instinct for death, but rather a psychological possibility which is socially mediated and can be reinforced by society—that is the love of death. The love of death is necrophilia, and Fromm contrasts necrophilia with biophilia, or love of life. These concepts of biophilia and necrophilia were adopted by Freire.

Fromm says,

> When life is characterised by growth in a structured,
> functional manner, the necrophilous person loves all that
> does not grow, that is mechanical. The necrophilous person
> is driven by the desire to transform the organic into the
> inorganic, to approach life mechanically, as if all living
> persons were things. . . . He loves control, and in the act of
> controlling he kills life.[6]

Fromm was interested in the mechanization of the human
experience as a process of modern industrial capitalism.
He was concerned that we would think of each other in
mechanistic ways and that we would come to love these
mechanistic ways of being and interacting in the world. He
saw these processes—in which we see ourselves and others as
things—as fundamentally alienating. Mechanization is what
industrial capitalism accomplishes, our fetishization of things,
of buying and selling, and our love of things and treatment of
others as things. That is, a necrophiliac relation to the world.

Freire also uses the concept of necrophilia in *Pedagogy of
the Oppressed*,

> Oppression—overwhelming control—is necrophilic; it is
> nourished by love of death, not life. The banking concept
> of education, which serves the interest of oppression, is also
> necrophilic. . . . It attempts to control thinking and action,
> leads men and women to adjust to the world, and inhibits
> their creative power.[7]

> The oppressed, who have been shaped by the death-affirming
> climate of oppression, must find through their struggle the
> way to life-affirming humanisation.[8]

In effect, Freire's resolution of the master–slave dialectic lies in
Fromm's biophilic humanization. Biophilia is the love of life, a
total orientation toward the preservation of life and the cycle
of life is that of union, birth, and growth. What is important

here, from Fromm's perspective, is the question of what social conditions produce biophilia/necrophilia. Necrophilia and biophilia are socially mediated. We can therefore create societies which are necrophilic, such as the modern society. To produce a society which is biophilic, freedom is required. However, Fromm's notion is that freedom both compels and repels us. We are enticed to seek freedom and desire to escape from it.

Fromm, like Freire, understood oppression as something which is both inward and outward; both in our psyche and in the social context. Fromm located oppression in fear: fear lodged deeply in our unconscious which can manifest in our fear of freedom. From this psychological perspective, Fromm is interested in the question of whether freedom can be a burden, even a burden too heavy to bear, and asks if we are attracted to our own submission. In *Pedagogy of the Oppressed*, Freire connects freedom to humanization,

> The oppressed, having internalized the image of the oppressor and adopted his guidelines, are fearful of freedom. Freedom would require them to eject this image and replace it with autonomy and responsibility. Freedom is acquired by conquest, not by gift. It must be pursued constantly and responsibly. Freedom is not an ideal located outside of man; nor is it an idea which becomes myth. It is rather the indispensable condition for the quest for human completion.[9]

From this statement, Freire goes on to describe the need for people to recognize the situation, causes, and techniques that produce oppression in society. The structures of domination, and how these are reproduced in the pedagogical relationship, therefore become the focus of *Pedagogy of the Oppressed*.

Alienation

Fromm draws on both Freud and Marx to understand alienation. In taking a psychoanalytic perspective, Fromm recognizes the material and social aspects of our alienation but emphasizes that alienation is also psychological. We are alienated from ourselves. Not only this, but we allow ourselves to be alienated. In fact, we can not only desire but also seek and accomplish this break from others. This is part of what it means to be human—to have the possibility to renounce one's freedom, to desire alienation. Fromm's resolution of this tension of freedom comes in love and work, which bind us together in purpose and action.

> There is only one possible, productive solution for the relationship of an individualized man with the world: his active solidarity with all men and his spontaneous activity, love and work, which unite him again with the world, not by primary ties but as a free and independent individual.[10]

Fromm says in his book *The Art of Loving*,

> If it is true, as I have tried to show, that love is the only sane and satisfactory answer to the problem of human existence, then any society which excludes, relatively, the development of love, must in the long run perish of its own contradiction with the basic necessities of human nature.[11]

Similarly, Freire says of love in *Pedagogy of the Oppressed*,

> Because love is an act of courage, not of fear, love is commitment to others. No matter where the oppressed are found, the act of love is commitment to their cause—the cause of liberation. And this commitment, because it is loving, is dialogical.[12]

For both Fromm and Freire love and work are the ontological opposite of alienation and oppression. This orientation toward the generative is evidence of their commitment to the humanist tradition and concern for the human condition and the criteria for the accomplishment of human freedom.

As Fromm says,

> Man is the end, and must never be used as a means; material production is for man, not man for material production; the aim of life is the unfolding of man's creative powers; the aim of history is a transformation of society into one governed by justice and truth.[13]

> Man's main task in life is to give birth to himself, to become what he potentially is. The most important product of his effort is his own personality.[14]

Both Freire and Fromm employ explanatory and normative accounts in their writings. However, a distinction can be made between Fromm and Freire in terms of their geographic positionalities. Fromm wrote from the Global North and in line with the tradition of Western thought, he presents his analysis in terms of the universal experience of (modern) man. Freire, whose first pedagogical experiences and writings emerge from the Global South, describes the interactional dynamics between illiterate peasants and authority figures in a situated reading. In this way, Freire's analysis is more closely related to epistemic tensions and power. For example, take Freire's concept of *cultural invasion,* in which "the invaders penetrate the cultural context of another group, in disrespect of the latter's potentialities; they impose their own view of the world upon those they invade and inhibit the creativity of the invaded by curbing their expression."[15] European colonization and the legacy of colonialism are the historical contexts of Freire's analysis of oppression. Because Fromm takes a psychoanalytical perspective on society, he deals less with concepts of culture or power differentials between knowledge systems. In this, Freire follows Marx more closely than he follows Fromm. Fromm was concerned with freedom in terms of uncovering internal conflicts within the individual psyche, a self-awareness which leads to freedom. Freire was more concerned, like Marx, with freedom as awareness of the political and economic circumstances of oppression.

This political focus connects back to the question of Freire's utopian inclination. Freire frames liberation as a pursuit, quest, and conquest which creates the condition for humanization. However, Freire does not entertain the notion that, having surmounted the dehumanizing situation of oppression, having jettisoned the internalized image of the oppressor, a person would still choose oppression. For Freire, the potential of those who are oppressed to become sub-oppressor rests on their false consciousness, "their perception of themselves as oppressed is impaired by their submersion in the reality of oppression."[16] Freire describes this "fear of freedom" as emerging from the "duality which has established itself in their innermost being" of the oppressed. The oppressed "discover that without freedom they cannot exist authentically. Yet, although they desire authentic existence, they fear it."[17] From Fromm's perspective, even when a person becomes fully aware of their oppression, they may still have psychological reasons to desire an escape from freedom. In this way, Fromm's escape from freedom describes how individuals and societies submit to and create the conditions for their own continued subjugation.

Fromm's rendering of the other's agency in his writings is minimal. For example, in *The Heart of Man*, he leads the reader through a thought exercise about a man's freedom of choice.[18] He describes the "almost unavoidable sequence" that if a man who sexually desires a woman asks her out for a drink "almost certainly he will find himself making love to her." As such, the choice to have intercourse is made by the man "when he invites her to have a drink . . . and not when he starts making love to her." At the later moment, for Fromm, the man is "no longer free" in the chain of decision-making. To the woman's desires and decisions, Fromm gives no interpretation.[19]

Freire takes a more positive view toward the agency of all actors in the dynamic interaction that emerges out of the freedom of the individual and agency of the other. Erich Fromm lived and taught in Mexico until 1974, when he retired to Muralto, Switzerland. He died of a heart attack in March 1980, five days before his eightieth birthday.

CHAPTER 2

Freire and hooks

Of the scholars whose works are presented in this book, bell hooks is the only one who wrote extensively about her interactions with Paulo Freire himself. She described their meeting at the University of Santa Cruz as "incredible," an experience that "made [her] a devoted student and comrade of Paulo's for life." At this meeting, from which hooks had been initially excluded, she hoped to have the chance to "interrogate Paulo Freire personally about the sexism in his work." Although others spoke against her for raising this critique, hooks described his reaction in this way:

> Paulo intervened to say that these questions were crucial and he addressed them. Truthfully, I loved him at this moment for exemplifying by his actions the principles of his work. So much would have changed for me had he tried to silence or belittle a feminist critique. And it was not enough for me that he owned his "sexism," I want to know why he had not seen that this aspect of earlier work be changed, be responded to in writing by him. And he spoke then about making more of a public effort to speak and write on these issues—this has been evident in his later work.[1]

For hooks, Freire's impact on her began years before, as she read his works and "learned new ways of thinking about social reality that were liberatory." Having lived through the struggle for racial desegregation in the south "without having a political language to articulate that process," hooks described Freire's work as giving her a language to articulate what became her revolutionary mantra:

> There was this one sentence of Freire's that became a revolutionary mantra for me: "We cannot enter the struggle as objects in order later to become subjects." Really, it is difficult to find words adequate to explain how this statement was like a locked door—and I struggled within myself to find the key—and that struggle engaged me in a process of critical thought that was transformative. This experience positioned Freire in my mind and heart as a challenging teacher whose work furthered my own struggle against the colonizing process—the colonizing mind-set.[2]

Rosa Bell Watkins gave birth to Gloria Jean Watkins, later known by her pen name bell hooks, in the small town of Hopkins, Kentucky, on September 25, 1952, during the racial apartheid era of Jim Crow in the United States. Rosa Bell worked cleaning the houses of white[3] people. Her husband, Veodis, worked as a janitor. When Watkins (hooks) was born, Rosa Bell had not yet finished high school. However, as a mother she supported the education of her children and Watkins credits her mother for instilling within her a love of learning. Under racial apartheid in Kentucky, Watkins attended racially segregated public elementary schools; in junior high and high school, she attended racially integrated public schools, before studying English at Stanford University. These different educational environments shaped Watkins's perspective on education, and she reflects on these experiences in her writing. During her time at Stanford, at age nineteen, Watkins authored her first book *Ain't I a Woman?: Black Women and Feminism*, which was published in 1981 under the name bell hooks. Watkins chose the name bell hooks after her great-grandmother Bell Blair Hooks, choosing lowercase letters as an act of subversion meant to place the focus of her work on her ideas rather than on her identity, a nod to her commitment to the feminist ethic of the 1960s and 1970s.

Even with this linguistic gesture away from her identity in her writing, bell hooks drew on her own autobiography extensively to explore themes of Blackness, antiracism, love, feminism, and capitalism. In 1983, she completed her PhD in literature with a dissertation on Black writer Toni Morrison, focusing on Morrison's characterization of Black females and exploring the Black female experience, including themes of self-hood and community. hooks made the point that writing is a political act with social relevance and that Morrison was able to maintain her autonomy as a writer without compromising on the aesthetic and imaginative art of literary expression. In her analysis of Morrison's *The Bluest Eye*, hooks elaborates the characters' anger, their internalization of colonial domination with its oppressor–oppressed structure, and the alienation that comes from Western society's emphasis on romantic love and physical beauty. hooks contextualized the experiences of Morrison's fictional characters with an incisive analysis of the oppressive desire for whiteness.

> The assumption that white skin, blond hair, and blue eyes are synonomous with beauty, and all else pales by comparison, has been part of the ideology of white supremacy and racism since its inception. Many black people have absorbed racist values and standards in their attempt to become like those in power. Whiteness is synonomous with privilege and power and that is what many black people have desired. That desire was articulated often indirectly through expressions of longing and desire for whiteness itself.[4]

hooks developed these themes in her later writing as well, not only in relation to literature and culture, but also in relation to teaching and pedagogy.

hooks was a storyteller. Her writing is vivid with stories from her own life. bell hooks wrote in a way that is very intimate, personal and even practical in terms of drawing on particular experiences and conversations, in particular with her students and colleagues. In this way, hooks made clear in her writing that her perspectives on the pedagogical possibilities for liberation are drawn from her own experiences. This choice to elaborate a critique of society as well as a feminist theory of radical pedagogy via narrative expression brings a vitality and accessibility to hooks's writing that cemented her position as educational inspirator. Freire also influenced the types of works hooks produced, for example, in the 1991 book *Breaking Bread* with Cornel West, the format of the book is dialogic. "One of my major mentors Paulo Freire, the Brazilian educator, always says that it is dialogue that is the true act of love between two subjects, and points out again and again, drawing on Che Guevara and others, that there can be no revolution without love."[5] hooks died of kidney failure in Kentucky on December 15, 2021, surrounded by her family.

Engaged Pedagogy

hooks herself was an educator. She wrote about teaching from a relational perspective that centers on the choices of activities that the teacher pursues in the classroom. hooks shares with Freire the perspective that starting with the personal experience of the students is liberatory.

> Once again, we are referring to a discussion of whether or not we subvert the classroom's politics of domination simply by using different material, or by having a different, more radical standpoint. Again and again, you and I are saying that different, more radical subject matter does not create a liberatory pedagogy, that a simple practice like including personal experience may be more constructively challenging than simply changing the curriculum.[6]

"Engaged pedagogy" refers to "a teaching strategy that aims to restore students' will to think, and their will to be fully self-actualized."[7] "Engaged pedagogy begins with the assumption that we learn best when there is an interactive relationship between student and teacher."[8] hooks was committed to the teachers' obligation to "take time to assess who we are teaching." She connects teaching and emotion, writing that engaged pedagogy requires "emotional awareness" and "emotional intelligence" to facilitate an environment where the students can develop their own sense of being.

hooks used the concept of *voice* to express something beyond the retelling of experience, "Coming to voice is not just the act of telling one's experience. It is using that telling strategically—to come to voice so that you can also speak freely about other subjects."[9] hooks invited her readers to develop the courage to speak freely and to pursue truth. She also brought together the notion of silencing the Other with a sense of "finishedness" as a type of censorship that assumes one knows what the other person thinks. This silencing is a form of dehumanization which does not leave room for dialogue and the necessary unfinishedness of learning, of not knowing what the other person would say or think, or how they might also change. In *Pedagogy of the Oppressed*, Freire discusses the need for unfinishedness as related to an education that it begins with a reflection on reality, which he calls "problem-posing education."

> Problem-posing education affirms men and women as beings in the process *of becoming*—as unfinished, uncompleted beings in and with a likewise unfinished reality. Indeed, in contrast to other animals who are unfinished, but not historical, people know themselves to be unfinished; they are aware of their incompletion. In this incompletion and this awareness lie the very roots of education as an exclusively human manifestation. The unfinished character of human beings and the transformational character of reality necessitate that education be an ongoing activity.[10]

In relation to voice and becoming, silence thus represents a foreclosure of the possibility for growth or solidarity. Both

Freire and hooks discuss the silencing which can happen in an authoritarian relation between the teacher and the student, of "talking back" or "speaking as an equal to an authority figure." It is from this vantage point that hooks described a liberatory pedagogy as one that transgresses boundaries—when an authoritarian silence is required, speaking is a transgression, one that is necessary to disrupt oppression. hooks thus tied liberation and transgression, talking about teachers and students transgressing the boundaries of race and class and gender, boundaries that have drawn lines of oppression.

hooks took her concept of pedagogical praxis in part from Freire, blending it also with the work of Buddhist monk Thich Nhat Hanh.

> Freire's work affirmed that education can only be liberatory when everyone claims knowledge as a field in which we all labor. That notion of mutual labor was affirmed by Thich Nhat Hanh's philosophy of engaged Buddhism, the focus on practice in conjunction with contemplation. His philosophy was similar to Freire's emphasis on "praxis"— action and reflection upon the world in order to change it. In his work Thich Nhat Hanh always speaks of the teacher as a healer. Like Freire, his approach to knowledge called on students to be active participants, to link awareness with practice. Whereas Freire was primarily concerned with the mind, Thich Nhat Hanh offered a way of thinking about pedagogy which emphasized wholeness, a union of mind, body, and spirit.[11]

Both Freire and hooks talk about their own processes of reflection—reflecting on their lives. There is a shared thematic of the experience of geographical distance from one's place of upbringing that brings new perspectives—for Freire in exile in Chile and for hooks as an undergraduate student in California.

Love and Rage

hooks's work reflects on emotions and bodies in relation to liberation. "In [the] work [of Fromm, King, and Merton], loving practice is not aimed at simply giving an individual greater life satisfaction; it is extolled as the primary way we end domination and oppression. This important politicization of love is often absent from today's writing."[12] She writes, "Living in faith means that we recognize, as our wise black female ancestors did, that we do have the power to decolonize our minds, invent ourselves and dwell in the spirit of love that is our true destiny."[13] "Love is our hope and our salvation."[14]

hooks displayed a facility with the expression of emotion by which she was able to evoke both a clear-sighted joy and rage. Freire also worked with the emotional aspects of liberation, writing, "The kind of education that does not recognize the right to express appropriate anger against injustice, against disloyalty, against the negation of love, against exploitation, and against violence fails to see the educational role implicit in the expression of these feelings."[15] Yet, he makes a distinction between anger and rage, writing, "However, it's important to stress the 'appropriateness' of this anger; otherwise it simply degenerates into rage and even hatred." hooks does not shy away from rage, she uses it "as a catalyst to develop critical Consciousness to come to full decolonized self-actualization."[16] Freire agrees,

I have a right to be angry, to show it and to use it as a motivational foundation for my struggle. . . . My right to be angry presupposes that the historical experience in which I participate tomorrow is not a given but a challenge and a problem. My just anger is grounded in any indignation in the face of the denial of the rights inherent in the very essence of the human condition. . . . To fight against what constitutes a denial of my own humanity.[17]

Reading Freire and hooks Together

Reading Freire through bell hooks offers the possibility to open his commentary on a range of issues not typically considered to be the core of Freire's work. This is possible because bell hooks herself wrote on such a range of topics. In *Teaching to Transgress*, hooks departed from Freire in her exploration of the *erotic* in relation to the pedagogic. While Freire discussed love, hooks rejected the western body–mind dualism and called attention to the body in the classroom—"What did one do with the body in the classroom." Another of hooks's insights relates to the representation of Black women in television and film, the consumption of white-produced media by Black audiences, the homogenization of white art, the appropriation of Black art by whites. hooks describes this as cultural invasion via media and cinema, in which the consumption of white culture in TV is "perpetuating and maintaining the values of white supremacy" through a "process of overt colonization." Similarly, Freire reflected on the relation between the media and a liberatory pedagogy:

> The whole area of communication comes immediately to mind. The knowledge of how to uncover hidden truths and how to demystify farcical ideologies, those seductive traps into which we easily fall. The knowledge of how to confront the enormous power of the media, the language of the television, which reduces to the same moment both past and present, suggesting that what has not yet happened has already come to pass. Even more than that, its power to generate a diversity of themes in its news bulletins without allowing the minimum of time for reflection on such a vast array of subjects. From news of the Miss Brazil contest we are whisked to an earthquake in China; from a scandal involving yet one more bank collapse due to unscrupulous bankers, we are hurried to a train crash in Zurich.

> The world is cut down to a village. Time is diluted. Yesterday becomes today. Tomorrow has already come. Everything is

done at high speed. In my view, it is extremely urgent that the power and effects of the media should be subjected to serious debate. As educators with open minds, we cannot ignore the television. We must, in fact, use it, but above all, we must discuss what is going on, what is being said and shown.[18]

Perhaps above all, Freire and hooks share the conviction that change is possible. Freire took hooks's feminist critique of his work in a humble way and sincerely requested that the scholars who would reinvent his work would do the same. Freire and hooks were both teachers, believing that people can learn and grow. In this, they did not give over to a deterministic fate that "the world is that way anyway," but shared the conviction that "It is imperative that we maintain hope even when the harshness of reality may suggest the opposite."[19]

CHAPTER 3

Freire and Dussel

Enrique Dussel begins writing his own biography with a description of the land—explaining the irrigation and how the river had dried up. Dussel was born in the province of Mendoza, Argentina, on Christmas Eve 1934, in a city that he says, "Garcia Marquez could have written about again in *100 years of Solitude*." His mother, "from an Italian family, was a militant catholic with a social sense"; his father was an "old-fashioned doctor" and a socialist of German descent, his great-grandfather arriving from Germany to Argentina in 1870. Dussel reflected on his father:

> At all hours of the day and night his patients arrived. I always remember how the people came to consult with him at night, in the wee-hours of the morning, he had no time for himself. When the road or the dirt track for the car ended, he continued by horse; he entered the most forgotten ranches of the desert, the poorest, even if they could not pay anything; with his hands he gave birth to all the children of the region for fifteen years; he founded the town's social clinic; there he practiced surgery; he had natural "clinical eye." It was an honor to be his son.

Dussel describes "happy years of a childhood among horses, cellars smelling of wine, sunbaked peasants." He studied philosophy as an undergraduate and then traveled to Europe where he completed doctoral degrees from the Complutense University of Madrid and from the Sorbonne in Paris. He studied Arabic and Hebrew in Israel before returning to Argentina in 1969. Between 1976 and 1983, he was increasingly the target of violence, including death threats, the bombing of his house, and sacking from the university. Like Freire, he became an exile because of a Latin American military dictatorship. Dussel escaped to Mexico in 1975 as a political exile, where he continued his work as a professor of philosophy.

Dussel's work is influenced by dependency theory and liberation theology. He has theorized extensively on the role of the Latin American Catholic church in social change and the epistemic consequences of Eurocentric modernity.

Pedagogics of Liberation

Dussel elaborates his understanding of the process of liberation using the concepts of the Other and Alterity. He defines domination and liberation on three levels: the erotic, pedagogic, and political.

The metaphor of the family is used to explain the development of political consciousness on these three levels.

> They are male-female, which becomes father-mother, parent-child, and brother-sister. The first is an erotic relationship, the second pedagogical, and the third political. And this applies even to the relationship of the totality of humankind before God, which is humankind's theological position, but always through the mediation of people, through "the poor, the orphan, or the widow," as the prophets say.

Dussel gives an intergenerational exploration of how political consciousness evolves within the family between the parents and the child. The child is something that emerges new. "A liberatory project is one where the father respects the child's alterity."[1]

The Other as child, youth, or the people is the absolute criterion of meta-physics and ethics: affirming the Other and serving him is the good act; negating the Other and dominating him is the evil act. The liberatory teacher permits the creative display of the Other. The preceptor masked behind "nature," "universal culture," and many other concealing fetishes is a false teacher, a sophist scientifist, the sage of the imperial system justifying the heroic conquistador's murders; he is the repressor.[2]

Freire shares a similar perspective on the parent–child relation:

The parent-child relationship in the home usually reflects the objective cultural conditions of the surrounding social structure. If the conditions which penetrate the home are authoritarian, rigid, and dominating, the home will increase the climate of oppression. As these authoritarian relations between parents and children intensify, children in their infancy increasingly internalize the paternal authority.[3]

Pedagogics, according to Dussel,

demands listening to the voice of the Other. In pedagogics the Other's voice signifies content revealing itself, and liberatory education can only begin with the revelation of the Other. The student reveals himself to the teacher; the teacher reveals himself to the disciple. If the child's voice, the voice of the youth and the people, is not heard by the father, the teacher, and the State, then liberatory education is impossible. Mutual listening sends, and essentially, the other receives (though clearly with diverse meanings for one party). This sending and receiving is the conditio sine qua non of pedagogical love (agapē) as extreme gratitude. But if speaking to the other is impossible, if transcending the ontic level of the expressive plane is like jumping on one's own shadow, all pedagogics will remain ontologically situated within the praxis of a pedagogics of domination where teachers and students can only speak with one another tautologically about "the Same," or that which the teacher is.[4]

In *Pedagogics of Liberation*, Dussel quotes from Freire, characterizing banking education which he opposed:

"(a) the teacher teaches and the students are taught; (b) the teacher knows everything and the students know nothing; (c) the teacher thinks and the students are thought about; (d) the teacher talks and the students listen—meekly; (e) the teacher disciplines and the students are disciplined; (f) the teacher chooses and enforces his choice, and the students comply; (g) the teacher acts and the students have the illusion of acting through the action of the teacher [. . .]."

Dussel then elaborates this in his own framing, saying, "We could continue the list of oppositions to infinity. What is certain is that the educator is the *schoolteacher I* constitutive of the pedagogical world, while the student is the *orphanic thing* which receives knowledge."[5]

Against Totality, Universalism, and Eurocentrism

Dussel gives a compelling critique of the Eurocentric center–periphery dynamic. Dussel argues that Europeans should understand they have positioned Europe as center in reference to a periphery of Others. While Freire acknowledges this as well in his later writings, especially *Pedagogy of Freedom* and *Pedagogy of Indignation*, Freire's earlier and more well-known works concentrate more on the notion that the oppressed recognize themselves as center. The aim of a pedagogy of the oppressed is that the oppressed would understand themselves as Subjects rather than Objects. Freire also indicates that this process of conscientization toward liberation is not a matter of the oppressors liberating the oppressed from domination but rather can only be accomplished when the oppressed liberate themselves.

Transmodernity

Dussel supports transmodernity as a liberatory alternative to Eurocentric modernity.

> The transmodern project is the mutual fulfillment of the "analectic" solidarity of center/periphery, woman/man, mankind/earth, western culture/peripheral postcolonial cultures, different races, different ethnicities, different classes. It should be noted here that this mutual fulfillment of solidarity does not take place by pure denial but rather by subsumption from alterity.[6]

Dussel's writing is practical. He gives concrete examples from modern reports, which he uses to ground his work in the material reality, rather than exercising a purely philosophical exploration of society and culture. Dussel's exploration of pedagogy follows the teacher-student relationship toward the maturation of the student in a relationship between equals. Dussel also offers a more gendered interpretation of equality, of male dominance in social interactions and of the social institution of the patriarchy, and the relation between a pedagogy of liberation and the enforcement of gender roles, including gendered subjugation.

A key insight from Dussel is that people are meant to move beyond the pedagogical relationship toward a relationship of equals, which he understands as the political relationship. Freire wrote that the pedagogical is always political. For Dussel, pedagogical relationships naturally assume a hierarchical dynamic, like the relationship between the mother and the child. At the point at which the teacher considers the child or the student as equal, they become colleagues. Freire distinguishes here between the teacher's authority, as a legitimate function of the teachers' responsibility, and authoritarianism, in which the teacher dominates the student. For Dussel, it is only as colleagues, as equals, that the relationship can become political. Dussel compares this to the relationship between Jesus and his disciples as one of siblings (brotherhood) in a relationship of equals.

For both Dussel and Freire, the quintessential element is the question of ethics—what we should and should not do. For both, there is a moral obligation for our actions to be benefiting the materiality of the poor. This is in line with the "preferential option for the poor," which is the core tenant of liberation theology.

CHAPTER 4

Freire and Fanon

Frantz Fanon was a direct influence on Paulo Freire. Fanon became a soldier and a doctor, a psychiatrist and a radical liberational militant. Fanon was born in 1925 in the French Caribbean colony of Martinique to a middle-class family. He was the fifth of eight children of Eléanore Médélice and her husband Félix Casimir. Fanon came of age during the Second World War, and his late adolescence and early adulthood were shaped by war and racism; when Fanon was fifteen, in 1940, France fell to the Nazis, and the French Navy were blocked on Martinique. The white French sailors took over the local government and Fanon described these men as behaving like "authentic racists."[1]

At age seventeen, Fanon enlisted in the French Free Forces. He served in Algeria and France. After the war Fanon returned to Martinique to complete his bachelor's degree and then traveled to France where he received his doctorate in psychiatry. During this time, he attended the lectures of philosopher Maurice Merleau-Ponty. He completed his first book, *Black Skin, White Masks*, in 1952 during his residency. He then moved to Algeria where he was chief of a psychiatric hospital. The Algerian revolution began in 1954, and Fanon joined the National Liberation Front.[2]

During this time, Fanon was responsible for treating both the people being tortured and the torturers. He saw how preference was given to the French for admission to the hospital, relative to the Muslim people of Algeria. Fanon realized he could not ethically continue in his position, and in 1956 he resigned from the hospital. In 1957 he was deported from Algeria, he was diagnosed with leukemia and sought treatment in the Soviet Union and then briefly in the United States, where he died in 1961 at the age of thirty-six. It is reported that Fanon's treatment was delayed when he arrived in the United States by eight days, and that this contributed to the deterioration of his condition and his untimely death. Fanon was buried in Algeria and his book *The Wretched of the Earth* was published in 1961.[3]

Blackness and Black Consciousness

Fanon made an immense contribution to the theorization of Black consciousness, using an approach that is both phenomenological and psychoanalytic. Fanon begins *Black Skin, White Masks* in a conversational tone, introducing his work with a profound question about humanity, racial identity and desire:

> Why write this book? No one has asked me for it.
> Especially those to whom it is directed.
> Well? Well, I reply quite calmly that there are too many idiots in this world. And having said it, I have the burden of proving it.
> Toward a new humanism . . .
> Understanding among men . . .
> Our colored brothers . . .
> Mankind, I believe in you.
> Race prejudice . . .
> To understand and to love . . .
> From all sides dozens and hundreds of pages assail
> me and try to impose their wills on me. But a single line would be enough. Supply a single answer and the color problem would be stripped of all its importance.

What does a man want?
What does the black man want?
At the risk of arousing the resentment of my colored
brothers, I will say that the black is not a man.
There is a zone of nonbeing, an extraordinarily sterile and
arid region, an utterly naked declivity where an authentic
upheaval can be born. In most cases, the black man lacks
the advantage of being able to accomplish this descent into
a real hell.[4]

Fanon describes the thesis of the book by saying, "In the
course of this essay we shall observe the development of an
effort to understand the black-white relation. The white man
is sealed in his whiteness. The black man in his blackness."
Fanon then clarifies the neuroticism of this relation, "There
is a fact: White men consider themselves superior to black
men. There is another fact: Black men want to prove to
white men, at all costs, the richness of their thought, the
equal value of their intellect." Fanon asks, "How do we
extricate ourselves?"

At the core of this question is one of humanization. "The
black man wants to be white. The white man slaves to reach
a human level." Fanon says, "The Negro is Enslaved by his
inferiority the white man enslaved by his superiority of like
behave in accordance with a neurotic orientation." Here we
see a connection with Freire, in terms of the dehumanization
of the oppressor and the oppressed through the oppressor's
actions. However, while Freire describes this relation in terms
of social and pedagogical dynamics, Fanon, approaching the
problem as a psychiatrist, was "led to consider their alienation
in terms of psychoanalytical classifications."

Fanon's exploration of racialized subjectivity and anti-
Blackness leads him to embrace a radical humanism: "Both
must turn their backs on the inhuman voices which were
those of their respective ancestors in order that authentic
communication be possible. Before it can adopt a positive
voice, freedom requires an effort at dis-alienation." Here again,

we see a link to Freire in the connection between subjectivity, humanization, and voice.

Freire saw racism, along with sexism and colonialism, as the most pervasive form of oppression.

Fanon's theorization of race, and specifically of the colonization of Black consciousness, can open up a deeper consideration of Freire's treatment of race and the racialization of both the oppressed and the oppressor.

Language

For Fanon, the question of language and power was specifically a question of knowing French. The French language is here connected to whiteness, "The Negro of the Antilles will be proportionately whiter—that is, he will come closer to being a real human being—in direct ratio to his mastery of the French language. . . . A man who has a language consequently possesses the world expressed and implied by that language. What we are getting at becomes plain: Mastery of language affords remarkable power." Fanon expands the question of language in relation to race and racialization, writing that "to speak a language is to participate in a world, to adopt a civilization." In this case, the language of the colonial oppressors.

Colonization

In 1953 when Fanon moved to Algeria, he made a shift in his writing toward a broader critique of colonialism. That shift is expressed in his book *The Wretched of the Earth*, which Freire cites in *Pedagogy of the Oppressed*. In fact, Freire added significantly to a draft of *Pedagogy of the Oppressed* for two reasons: first, that his publisher wanted an additional chapter with more pedagogical examples for practice, and second, to incorporate what Freire had read in Fanon's *The Wretched of the Earth*.

Freire cites Fanon:

> Submerged in reality, the oppressed cannot perceive clearly the "order" which serves the interests of the oppressors whose image they have internalized. Chafing under the restrictions of this order, they often manifest a type of horizontal violence, striking out at their own comrades for the pettiest reasons.

> The colonized man will first manifest this aggressiveness which has been deposited in his bones against his own people. This is the period when the niggers beat each other up, and the police and magistrates do not know which way to turn when faced with the astonishing waves of crime in North Africa. . . . While the settler or the policeman has the right the livelong day to strike the native, to insult him and to make him crawl to them, you will see the native reaching for his knife at the slightest hostile or aggressive glance cast on him by another native; for the last resort of the native is to defend his personality vis-a-vis his brother.[5]

Fanon says,

> The colonist is not content with physically limiting the space of the colonized, i.e., with the help of his agents of law and order. As if to illustrate the totalitarian nature of colonial exploitation, the colonist turns the colonized into a kind of quintessence of evil. Colonized society is not merely portrayed as a society without values. The colonist is not content with stating that the colonized world has lost its values or worse never possessed any. The "native" is declared impervious to ethics, representing not only the absence of values but also the negation of values. He is, dare we say it, the enemy of values. In other words, absolute evil.

In this way, Fanon understands that colonization is not only an economic, geographic, and material process, it is also a psychological process. "Colonialism forces the colonized to constantly ask the question: 'Who am I in reality?'" It is here that Fanon suggests that a Marxist reading should be "stretched" to include a framework in which the ruling class is also, and always remains, "foreign" while the Indigenous populations become "the others."

Colonialism led to systematic, structured inequality. Fanon emphasizes that this is not an accident—colonialism is not by chance, and it is not violent by chance; this is the nature of colonial power and domination. Fanon writes, "[t]his compartmentalized [colonized] world . . . this world divided in two, is inhabited by different species." He goes on, "Looking at the immediacies of the colonial context, it is clear that what divides this world is first and foremost what species, what race one belongs to. In the colonies the economic infrastructure is also a superstructure. The cause is effect: You are rich because you are white, you are white because you are rich."

Fanon sets out an agenda for decolonization and liberation:

The violence which governed the ordering of the colonial world, which tirelessly punctuated the destruction of the indigenous social fabric, and demolished unchecked the systems of reference of the country's economy, lifestyles, and modes of dress, this same violence will be vindicated and appropriated when, taking history into their own hands, the colonized swarm into the forbidden cities. To blow the colonial world to smithereens is henceforth a clear image within the grasp and imagination of every colonized subject. To dislocate the colonial world does not mean that once the borders have been eliminated there will be a right of way between the two sectors. To destroy the colonial world means nothing less than demolishing the colonist's sector, burying it deep within the earth or banishing it from the territory.

Liberation

For Fanon, liberation is connected to consciousness. To be liberated is to reject individualism.

> The colonized intellectual learned from his masters that the individual must assert himself. The colonialist bourgeoisie hammered into the colonized mind the notion of a society of individuals where each is locked in his subjectivity, where wealth lies in thought. But the colonized intellectual who is lucky enough to bunker down with the people during the liberation struggle, will soon discover the falsity of this theory. Involvement in the organization of the struggle will already introduce him to a different vocabulary. "Brother," "sister," "comrade."[6]

Fanon says the "colonized intellectual" has been "pulverized by colonialist culture," which evokes Freire's statement "The struggle begins with men's recognition that they have been destroyed."[7]

Fanon describes the relationships between political consciousness and liberation through a dialectical process.

> People must know where they are going and why. The politician should be aware that the future will remain bleak as long as the people's consciousness remains rudimentary, primary, and opaque. We, African politicians, must have very clear ideas about our peoples' situation. But this lucidity must remain deeply dialectical. The awakening of the people as a whole will not be achieved overnight; their rational commitment to the task of building the nation will be simple and straightforward; first of all, because the methods and channels of communication are still in the development stages; secondly, because the sense of time must no longer be that of the moment or the next harvest but rather that of the rest of the world; and finally,

because the demoralization buried deep within the mind by colonization is still very much alive.[8]

In terms of liberation, Fanon was also attentive to the practicalities of liberation in Africa, of leadership, and of the material realities of political liberation from the colonists. Fanon made three distinctions within the population: the colonizers or Western bourgeois, the "national bourgeois" or "colonized bourgeois," that is the elite of the Indigenous population, and finally the Indigenous proletariat. This tripartite distinction may be a point where Fanon departs from Freire. Fanon is careful to elaborate the role and the shortcomings of the national bourgeois in the process of decolonization. Yet he doesn't spend as much time discussing the role of the Indigenous proletariat in achieving their own liberation. He spends more time discussing their support for the revolution. Using the Hegelian master–slave dialectic, Freire is clear that the oppressed will never be liberated by the oppressors or sub-oppressors; the oppressed hold the key to liberation, both for themselves and for their oppressors.

On Violence and Education

There are two points of departure for further consideration of Fanon and Freire worth highlighting briefly. As discussed earlier, a fundamental overlap in their writings are themes of humanization and liberation. Fanon's consideration of violence theorizes the connection between liberation and violent revolution. Fanon understood that the colonizers' violence can only be met with violence; this is the only rational option. Fanon and Freire both understood that colonialism in its very nature is violent.

As Freire wrote:

Every relationship of domination, of exploitation, of oppression is by definition violent, whether or not the violence is expressed by drastic means. In such a relationship, dominator and dominated alike are reduced to things- the former dehumanized by an excess of power, the latter by a lack of it. And things cannot love.[9]

Yet Fanon believed that greater violence is necessary to overcome domination. Fanon's experience with the use of torture as a psychological practice of the destruction of the other person's humanity moved him to see psychological violence as irremediable by symbolic means: torture cannot be stopped with words but only by physical means. This stance raises the question of the legitimate use of violence and the relationship between humanization and violence.

CHAPTER 5

Freire and Gramsci

Giuseppina Marcias, known as Peppina, gave birth to the fourth of her seven children, Antonio Gramsci, on January 22, 1891, in Ales Sardinia. Known as Nino to his family, Gramsci's childhood was marked by physical and financial turmoil. Peppina was a bright woman from an established Sardinian family, and Francesco, her husband, was of Greek-Albanian descent. Francesco worked as an administrator in the local civil service. Gramsci was ill for much of his life; his poor health was exacerbated by political persecution and imprisonment. He was treated for depression and physical disabilities, including Potts disease and arteriosclerosis.[1]

> When I was a child the village boys never came near me except to make fun of me. I was almost always alone. Sometimes they might find me near them and set upon me, and not only with insults. One day they started throwing stones at me more viciously than usual, with the malice peculiar to children and the downtrodden. I lost my temper and threw stones back, so fiercely that they fled. From that day they let me be.[2]

Gramsci became head of the Italian Communist Party and was arrested and imprisoned in 1926. While in prison he wrote a series of letters giving a critique of Marx and exploring the failure of the Italians left to generate sufficient political support. Gramsci was interested in mapping and identifying the reproduction of dominant ideologies which govern institutions and the reproduction of support for the state, and how the state and civil society produce and maintain consent to the class hierarchies of capitalist society. Gramsci's health deteriorated while in prison and he died in 1937 in Rome at age forty-six. Freire was introduced to Gramsci's work by Marcela Gajardo during his period of exile in Chile.[3]

Praxis

Gramsci's use of the term "praxis" in his writings is somewhat diffuse. In one sense, he used the term "praxis" as a placeholder to indicate his orientation toward understanding social relations described by Marx. In the introduction to the prison notebooks, others have noted that because Gramsci was writing in prison, he had to be careful with the language that he chose. Gramsci describes the philosophy of praxis, saying:

> the basic innovation introduced by the philosophy of praxis into the science of politics and of history is the demonstration that there is no abstract "human nature," fixed and immutable (a concept which certainly derives from religious and transcendentalist thought), but that human nature is the totality of historically determined social relations, hence an historical fact which can, within certain limits, be ascertained with the methods of philology and criticism.[4]

Gramscian praxis is, therefore, "'materialism' perfected by the work of speculative philosophy itself and fused with humanism."[5]

> In a sense, moreover, the philosophy of praxis is a reform and a development of Hegelianism; it is a philosophy that has been liberated (or is attempting to liberate itself)

from any unilateral and fanatical ideological elements; it is consciousness full of contradictions, in which the philosopher himself, understood both individually and as an entire social group, not only grasps the contradictions, but posits himself as an element of the contradiction and elevates this element to a principle of knowledge and therefore of action.[6]

Unlike Gramsci's rather opaque, adaptable use of the term "praxis," Freire's notion of praxis is often interpreted by contemporary educators as simply the connection between theory and practice or the realization of theory in practice. However, Freire's understanding of praxis is intimately tied to social transformation through a process of reflection and action:

One of the gravest obstacles to the achievement of liberation is that oppressive reality absorbs those within it and thereby acts to submerge human beings consiousness. Functionally, oppression is domesticating. To no longer be prey to its force, one must emerge from it and turn upon it. This can be done only by means of the praxis: reflection and action upon the world in order to transform it.[7]

Freire interprets Marx and Engles, saying:

Making "real oppression more oppressive still by adding to it the realization of oppression" corresponds to the dialectical relation between the subjective and the objective. Only in this interdependence is an authentic praxis possible, without which it is impossible to resolve the oppressor-oppressed contradiction. To achieve this goal, the oppressed must confront reality critically, simultaneously objectifying and acting upon that reality. A mere perception of reality not followed by this critical intervention will not lead to a transformation of objective reality—precisely because it is not a true perception.[8]

Hegemony

Gramsci's elaboration of the concept of hegemony is perhaps his most lasting impact on social and political theory. Gramsci uses the concept of hegemony to explain how the bourgeois reproduce power not only through the apparatus of the state but also through the maintenance of dominant social and cultural ideals. The exercise of hegemony is characterized by the appearance of consent.

"The 'normal' exercise of hegemony . . . is characterized by the combination of force and consent, which balance each other reciprocally, without force predominating excessively over consent."[9]

Freire also uses the concept of hegemony, for example, to explain the oppressor's rationale for the practice of divide and rule:

> As the oppressor minority subordinates and dominates the majority, it must divide it and keep it divided in order to remain in power. The minority cannot permit itself the luxury of tolerating the unification of the people, which would undoubtedly signify a serious threat to their own hegemony. Accordingly, the oppressors halt by any method (including violence) any action which in even incipient fashion could awaken the oppressed to the need for unity.[10]

Freire references hegemony as the dominance which the elites work to preserve through anti-dialogical action. Gramsci distinguishes between the hegemonic and the subaltern or subordinate groups in society, in a similar Hegelian style to the distinction that Freire makes between the oppressors and the oppressed. The Hegelian master–slave dialectic appears as central in Freire's work, as well as in the work of many critical scholars following Marx.

The Organic Intellectual

When Gramsci considers how political change happens, and how change *can* happen, he describes the work of intellectuals from the proletariat—the organic intellectual—who can articulate and represent the political perspectives of the proletariat. Gramsci's idea of "intellectuals" refers to the strata of people who work in any field, who "give [the social group] homogeneity and an awareness of its own function not only in the economic but also in the social and political field." He gives an example of the capitalist entrepreneur as a type of intellectual, who

> must have a certain technical capacity, not only in the limited sphere of his activity and initiative but in other spheres as well, at least in those which are closest to economic production. He must be an organiser of masses of men; he must be an organiser of the "confidence" of investors in his business, of the customers for his product, etc.[11]

Gramsci describes the evolution of the traditional intellectuals, the "ecclesiastics who for a long time (for a whole phase of history, which is partly characterised by this very monopoly) held a monopoly of a number of important services: religious ideology, that is the philosophy and science of the age, together with schools, education, morality, justice, charity, good works, etc."[12] which then evolved into the "*noblesse de robe,* with its own privileges, a stratum of administrators, etc., scholars and scientists, theorists, non- ecclesiastical philosophers, etc."[13]

Gramsci connects the development of the intellectual stratum of society directly to education: "School is the instrument through which intellectuals of various levels are elaborated."[14]

Freire wrote in a similar way about the production of intellectuals:

> I am convinced that it is easier to create a new type of intellectual-forged in the unity between practice and theory, manual and intellectual work-than to reeducate an elitist intellectual. When I say it is easier, I do not discount the validity of such reeducation when it does occur.[15]

However, Freire orients his solution in the pedagogical methods that are used. "The preparation of cadres with a popular rather than an elitist orientation can be carried on not only outside but inside the country. Needs of learners can be defined in close relation to new pedagogical methods." For Freire, this tension between the intellectuals of the elite and of the people is also about the colonialism present in the methods of education and knowledge production, especially when writing from Guinea-Bissau.

Freire and Gramsci on Education

Peter Mayo has written extensively on the relevance of Gramsci's thought to education, suggesting that "Gramsci's entire project in the prison writings, centring on the notion of hegemony. . . is an educational project."[16] Although Freire's later writings discuss the public education of children and Gramsci elaborated his views on the curricular aspects of basic education, including his perspective on the teaching of Greek and Latin in schools and the relationship between the education of the youth and the reproduction of hegemony, both Freire and Gramsci have strong applications for adult education. Freire's experience and inspiration for his pedagogy come from his experience as an educator of adults.[17] Mayo has extended this connection and analysis of Gramsci's relevance to adult education, drawing Freire and Gramsci together in an exploration of a radical and transformative adult education. In this way, the synergies between the two critical theorists continues in contemporary scholarship on a range of issues related to education, including history, agency, social movements, cultural production and the role of the adult educator.[18]

CHAPTER 6

Freire and Habermas

This brief biography of Jürgen Habermas begins with his own ambivalence about the relationship between biography and scholarship.

> The ideas of such a classical thinker are like the molten core beneath the volcano that has deposited biographical rings of hardened lava. The great thinkers of the past whose works have stood the test of time impress this image upon us. By contrast, we, the many living philosophers—who are in any case more professors of philosophy—are merely the contemporaries of our contemporaries. And the less original our ideas are the more they remain bound to the context from which they emerged. At times, indeed, they are no more than an expression of the biography from which they spring.

Grete Habermas gave birth to Jürgen, the second of her three children, on June 18, 1929, in North-Rhine Westphalia, Germany.[1] Grete's husband Ernst Habermas served as director of the Cologne Bureau of Trade and Industry. Habermas was born with a cleft palate, and when asked to discuss the relation between his biography and his philosophy, he described how this shaped his experiences.

I shall begin with my early childhood with an operation I underwent directly after I was born. I do not believe that this surgery, as one might suppose, enduringly shook my faith in the world around me. However, that intervention may well have awakened the feelings of dependence and vulnerability and the sense of the relevance of our interactions *with others*. . . . Needless to say I can no longer remember the first operation on my cleft palate but when I had to undergo the repeat upper of the operation at the age of five—in other words a time that I remember clearly—it undoubtedly sharpened my awareness of the deep dependence of one person on others. At any rate, this heightened sensitivity to the social nature of human beings led me to those philosophical approaches that emphasize the intersubjective constitution of the human mind . . . the intuitive sense of the deeply rooted reciprocal dependence of one person on another finds expression in an image of the human being's place in the world.[2]

Habermas speaks of his schooling:

I remember the difficulties I encountered when I tried to make myself understood in class or during break while speaking with my nasal articulation and distorted pronunciation of which I was completely unaware. I had left the haven of family life and its familiar surroundings and had to find my feet in an anonymous domain failures of communication direct our attention to an otherwise unobtrusive intermediary world of symbols that cannot be grasped like physical objects only when communication fails do we become aware of the medium of linguistic communication as a shared stratum without which individual existence would also be impossible. We invariably find ourselves within the element of language only someone who speaks can remain silent only because we are inherently connected with one another can we feel lonely or isolated.

Like many of the other German scholars of the Frankfurt school writing in the early twentieth century, Habermas was very interested in understanding how a society can behave irrationally. One thread in Habermas's work is his trying to understand Nazism and his family's participation in the National Socialist Party and their "bourgeois adaptation to a political situation with which one did not fully identify, but which one didn't seriously criticize either."[3] Habermas was enrolled in the Hitler Youth at the age of fourteen. He was very much impacted by 1945 Nazi Germany, when at the age of sixteen the extent of the Holocaust became more fully known to the German people.

> Overnight as it were the society in which we had led what had seemed to be a halfway normal everyday life and the regime governing it were exposed as pathological and criminal through this experience the confrontation with the legacy of the Nazi past became a fundamental theme of my adult political life my interest in political progress spurred by this concern with the past became focused on conditions of life that escaped the false alternative.

That experience led him as a philosopher to explore a Kantian understanding of reason and rationality, and to a reinterpretation of Marx. It also led him to give a critique of the German philosopher Martin Heidegger, who was himself a Nazi. As Habermas put it, "the conceptual triad of public space, discourse and reason in fact has dominated my work as a scholar and my political life. Any such obsession has biographical roots."

Intersubjectivity

Habermas was interested in questions of morality and the connection between the rational and the moral. He was very much influenced by Kant's interpretation of reason, but

Habermas thought that there was something missing when reason was described as either an objective truth which could be found through logic or a subjective truth which existed only in the minds of people. Habermas took what is called the "linguistic turn" and understood that reason is neither objective nor subjective but *intersubjective*. People define what can be considered as reasonable and rational through what Habermas called "communicative action," a more expansive way of saying talking—that also includes communication that is not only verbal. For Habermas, our morality, and the possibility for emancipation, comes not through adherence to an objective reason, or through participation in systems of rationalization, but through communication. Likewise, Freire also saw the primacy of language and dialogue as part of emancipation, and he also used the idea of intersubjectivity to describe the difference between oppressive action and revolutionary action.[4]

Communicative Action

In 1981, Habermas published his book *The Theory of Communicative Action*. Habermas suggests that we accomplish reason through what he calls *communicative action*. By this he means that because reason is not simply objective nor simply subjective but intersubjective and produced in interaction, rationality is a product of communication. For Habermas, language is the primary mode of communication— but his use of the concept of *communicative action* widens the scope of communication beyond simply talking. The accomplishment of rationality through communication means that our communication has ethical implications on the level of relationships between individuals and at the level of the society. Habermas's concern for the ethical implications of the relation between reason and communication led him to theorize about how democracy is accomplished through communicative action. He developed the theory of the public sphere, a site in civil society where it is possible to debate, argue, and, through communicative action, agree on what is rational.

The concern of the ethical, for mutual recognition, for public dialogue and democracy, is one of the key places where Freire and Habermas overlap. For both writers, it is through mutual recognition that we can come to dialogue. Habermas makes a distinction between the spoken and the written word—between *dialogue*, which is spoken, and *discourse*, which is written. Habermas favors written word, because he sees the written word as the space where debate can happen, where ideas can be argued and tested. This is interesting from a Freirean perspective for two reasons, first because Freire worked in a very conversational way and teaching often is an interactional dialogue of speaking with the student. Second, Freire's work began with the political necessity of the peasant's ability to participate in discourse (the written word). Freire's literacy campaign was aimed at broadening the political participation of the Brazilian peasants by teaching them to read and write. For both Freire and Habermas, there is a connection between reading the word, political activity, and political consciousness. Dialogue is mutually understood as a moral relation—and it is through this relation, in which we recognize one another and reflect on our interaction, that we can achieve reconciliation through love.

Between Freire and Habermas

Raymond Allen Morrow and Carlos Alberto Torres have written extensively about the synergies between Freire and Gramsci, elaborating the "dialogical and developmental subject" as the core of their complementary approaches.[56] These synergies can be mapped across the ontological, epistemic and methodological approaches used by Freire and Gramsci. Habermas shares with Freire a commitment to the possibility for truly just, moral, and ethically honest social relations. One of the critiques of Habermas is therefore the same critique given to Freire, which is that he is a utopian thinker. Freire and Habermas also minimally address issues of race and gender. The corporeality of rationalization, that is, the relationship of the body to communicative action, is not sufficiently addressed in Habermas's work. This is especially apparent in Habermas's lack of attention to forms of violence. He acknowledges that language can be a form of violence but does not theorize physical violence as communicative action—physical violence is therefore irrational in that it cannot constitute communicative action. Samantha Asheden has explored how Habermas "rationalizes and attempts to eliminate violence from his consideration of law and language."[7] Here Habermas has much in common with Freire, because Freire frames oppression as a systemic domination accomplished habitually in symbolic ways—ways that the oppressed accept or are rationalized through domination to be tolerable. The solution for Freire to overcome this symbolic violence and unjust social positioning is not primarily through physical violence—but through dialogue and love.

Freire and Habermas share a grounding in the Hegelian master–slave dialectic as well as in Marxist theory of praxis. Habermas rejects the ontological distinction between the master and the slave and says rather that they are generated linguistically through communicative action in a certain intersubjective rationality which creates both the master and slave as such, as well as the attendant meanings and rationalities for their relation. Freire also wants to disrupt the master–slave dialectic in the social environment, yet his solution is one of praxis—of reconciliation. Freire offers a practical and explicitly *pedagogical* alternative to how people can be emancipated from the subordinate position through *conscientization*. Conscientization is an educational process by which people become aware of their political position within an oppressive cultural system. It is interesting also here to recall the religious undertones of Freire's writing, in which his ontological answer to the master–slave dialectic may be understood as a vocation toward humanization.

There is also a synergy between Habermas's understanding of the lifeworld being colonized by instrumental rationality and Freire's understanding of education being colonized by the banking mode of teaching. The metaphor that Freire chooses to use to explain banking education is a technical understanding of learning: a systematic and institutional metaphor. Banking education is a kind of rationalization of learning in which the lifeworld of the students is colonized by an instrumental rationality which happens through the education system. Banking education creates norms that enjoy legitimate power without a legitimate political process of consensus making through dialogue, without a recognition of the humanity of the peasants. Habermas refers to the ways that technical systems encroach on our daily lives.

When stripped of their ideological veils, the imperatives of autonomous subsystems make their way into the life world from the outside like colonial masters coming into a tribal society and force a process of assimilation upon it. The diffused perspectives the local culture cannot be sufficiently coordinated to permit the play of the metropolis and the world market to be grasped from the periphery.

Habermas elaborates alienation and false consciousness, Marxian concepts which Freire also uses, as part of the phenomenon of the colonization of the lifeworld by this technical rationality of systems which are instrumental rather than communicative. The implication is that while communicative action can be moral, technical rationality, because it governs systems of instrumentality, is incapable of communicating ethics.

CHAPTER 7

Freire and Fraser

Nancy Fraser was born on May 20, 1947, in Maryland. She grew up in Baltimore during the period of racial segregation, and she describes growing up during the fight for desegregation as being formative. American assimilation was part of her own family story, a mythology she identified with the "bad girls" of the family and being a rebel.

I come from a family on my father's side of Eastern European Jews (Poland and Lithuania, primarily). My father was born in the USA but his parents were immigrants. That was a somewhat conventional family, very oriented toward assimilating to American life. My mother's side is somewhat more complicated because her mother's side were of Irish Catholic descent, and she was born and raised on the eastern shore of Maryland, a somewhat isolated, inward-looking, even xenophobic region oriented toward farming and fishing. I very much identified with the women on this side of the family, for many of them were rebels and bad girls, including my great-grandmother who ran off with a Jewish peddler. My grandmother was the fruit of this union though they never married, so on this side of the family there were a series of female rebellions with which I identified very strongly. I have a whole personal mythology about this "bad girl" strain in my family, which tapped into a certain orientation toward revolt and feminism "avant la lettre."[1]

Fraser describes herself as being "kind of in rebellion for much of my life," a rebellion that for her "took the form of wanting to become fiercely intellectually serious in contrast to the milieu" which she considered "unserious." Fraser then studied Greek and Latin as an undergraduate at Bryn Mawr, where she soon developed an interest in philosophy. Bryn Mawr is a historically women's college, and there Fraser became part of the Students for a Democratic Society during the US involvement in the Vietnam War. Fraser was an activist and a self-described "non-orthodox Marxist" raised with a Jewish identity. She earned her PhD in philosophy in New York, and although she identifies with "Critical Theory and Hegelian Marxism," she describes herself as "someone who wants to update the Frankfurt School tradition of critical theory."[2] Here we see a connection with Freire, because his work can also be read as an extension of Hegelian Marxism.[3]

Fraser's work has been concerned with the practicalities of political and social emancipation of women. Her analysis is attentive to the current and historical possibilities for political participation, developing analytical frames and ways of understanding political participation which not only explain the current situation but also map an agenda for achieving greater justice within society. She does this, for example, in her tripartite understanding of the relationship between *representation*, *recognition*, and *redistribution*. These three represent the political, social, and economic aspects of power.

Freire has been concerned with the ontological question of how the oppressed can realize the "vocation to be more fully human," describing the dynamics between oppressor and oppressed within the classroom. Fraser's concern turns toward societal material reality of the paradigms which have created the questions that we are asking, for example questions of how justice is understood in relation to particular notions of the state, how citizenship is understood in relation to the Keynesian-Westphalian notion of the state as a national entity, and how has globalization changed the possibilities for framing citizenship, public debate, and public participation. Freire eventually came to talk more about the state in his later writings, but his primary concerns emerged from the interactional and pedagogical processes by which oppression is reproduced. However, Freire and Fraser share a commitment to democracy and political participation through recognition.

(Mis)recognition

One of Fraser's core contributions is her theorization of the ways that a lack of recognition affects democratic possibilities in society.

> To be misrecognized, in my view, is not simply to be thought ill of, looked down on, or devalued in others' conscious attitudes or mental beliefs. It is rather to be denied the status of a full partner in social interaction and prevented from participating as a peer in social life—not as a consequence of a distributive inequity (such as failing to receive one's fair share of resources or "primary goods"), but rather as a consequence of institutionalized patterns of interpretation and evaluation that constitute one as comparatively unworthy of respect or esteem. When such patterns of disrespect and disesteem are institutionalized, for example, in law, social welfare, medicine, and/or popular culture, they impede parity of participation, just as surely as do distributive inequities. The resulting harm is in either case all too real. In my conception, therefore, misrecognition is an institutionalized social relation, not a psychological state.[4]

Fraser here elaborates the idea of *recognition* from Hegel, from whom Freire also draws to discuss how the oppressed can fail to recognize themselves as oppressed. Freire cites Hegel in *Pedagogy of the Oppressed:*
As Hegel testifies:

it is solely by risking life that freedom is obtained the individual who has not staked his or her life may know. Be recognized as a person but he or she has not attained the truth of this recognition as an independent self-consciousness.

Men and women rarely admit their fear of freedom openly, however, tending rather to camouflage it—sometimes unconsciously—by presenting themselves as defenders of freedom. They give their doubts and misgivings an air of profound sobriety, as befitting custodians of freedom.[5]

Freire also talks about recognition in terms of dialogue.

Dialogue, as the encounter of those addressed to the common task of learning and acting, is broken if the parties (or one of them) lack humility. How can I dialogue if I always project ignorance onto others and never perceive my own? How can I dialogue if I regard myself as a case apart from others—mere "its" in whom I cannot recognize other "I"s? How can I dialogue if I consider myself a member of the in-group of "pure" men, the owners of truth and knowledge, for whom all non-members are "these people" or "the great unwashed"? How can I dialogue if I start from the premise that naming the world is the task of an elite and that the presence of the people in history is a sign of deterioration, thus to be avoided? How can I dialogue if I am closed to—and even offended by—the contribution of others? How can I dialogue if I am afraid of being displaced, the mere possibility causing me torment and weakness?[6]

Participatory Parity

In a just society, Fraser suggests, all members can participate as peers, on par with one another:

> The conception of justice I propose centres on the principle of parity of participation. According to this principle, justice requires social arrangements that permit all (adult) members of society to interact with one another as peers. For participatory parity to be possible, at least two conditions must be satisfied. First, the distribution of material resources must be such as to ensure participants' independence and "voice." This "objective" condition precludes forms and levels of economic dependence and inequality that impede parity of participation. Precluded, therefore, are social arrangements that institutionalize deprivation, exploitation, and gross disparities in wealth, income, and leisure time, thereby denying some people the means and opportunities to interact with others as peers. In contrast, the second condition for participatory parity is "intersubjective." It requires that institutionalized patterns of cultural value express equal respect for all participants and ensure equal opportunity for achieving social esteem. This condition precludes institutionalized value patterns that systematically depreciate some categories of people and the qualities associated with them. Precluded, therefore, are institutionalized value patterns that deny some people the status of full partners in interaction—whether by burdening them with excessive ascribed "difference" or by failing to acknowledge their distinctiveness. Both conditions are necessary for participatory parity. Neither, alone, is sufficient.[7]

For Fraser, "parity is not a matter of numbers. Rather, it is a qualitative condition, the condition of being a peer, of being on a par with others, of interacting with them on an equal footing."[8] As a feminist scholar, Fraser gives specific examples related to gender,

In the case of gender disparity in political representation, then, I assume that what is required is not only the deinstitutionalization of androcentric value hierarchies, but also the restructuring of the division of labour to eliminate women's "double shift," which constitutes a formidable distributive obstacle to their full participation in political life.[9]

Fraser's notion of participatory parity can raise interesting questions for Freire, including his perspectives on gender, on the types of labor that are valued, and on how the rhythms of certain types of labor exclude or form an obstacle to participation in political life and adult education.

Discursive Contestation

Like Freire, Fraser is interested in the emancipatory project. Reading Fraser and Freire together can open the question of the horizon of liberation. Freire's work has been taken internationally describing a colonial dynamic between the peasants and the dominant class—a work emergent from Brazil—but a dynamic at work in all of the post-colonies and any context in which groups of people have been politically and socially and economically marginalized, deprived of recognition as equal human beings with equal possibilities for social participation. Fraser speaks in her later work about globalization and the question of the public sphere in relation to the dissolution or the evolution of the state and global governance. She gives the example of the women's rights movement as part of the emergence of a global public sphere. Reading Freire through Fraser can lead to a more comprehensive consideration of how Freire's critical theory could be read in light of globalization and the ongoing political, social, and economic dynamics between the Global South and the Global North.

Fraser continually illuminates the challenges for the liberal elite to embrace a radical emancipatory and liberatory position. Taken together with Freire, we are reminded of his position that the oppressors can never liberate themselves but can become conscious of their position as oppressor and work in solidarity with the oppressed.

> This, then, is the great humanistic and historical task of the oppressed: to liberate themselves and their oppressors as well. The oppressors, who oppress, exploit, and rape by virtue of their power, cannot find in this power the strength to liberate either the oppressed or themselves. Only power that springs from the weakness of the oppressed will be sufficiently strong to free both.[10]

Like Freire, Fraser understands her work in a dialogic way. Speaking of her exchanges with Butler, Young, and other feminist scholars, Fraser writes, "In fact, I'm the sort of thinker who works dialogically, in and through debates and exchanges. (Remember that both Feminist Contentions [Benhabib et al. 1994] and Redistribution or Recognition? [Fraser and Honneth 2003] have this form.) I often don't know what I really think about something until I've encountered others who (it turns out) think differently."[11]

Like for Freire, who through dialogue developed his consciousness about gender, there can be seen in Fraser's work also an evolution in her thinking. In the 1990s, she writes about the tensions between redistribution and recognition and the politics of redistribution in the politics of recognition. By the 2000s, she begins to articulate a third aspect, following Max Weber in making a distinction between the cultural or social, the political and economic, "Representation, accordingly, constitutes a third, political dimension of social justice, alongside the (economic) dimension of redistribution and the (cultural) dimension of recognition."[12]

CHAPTER 8

Freire and Bakhtin

Varvara Zakharovna Bakhtin[1] gave birth to Mikhail Bakhtin on November 17, 1895, in Oryol, Russia. The family was of Russian nobility, and Bakhtin's father Mikhael worked as a bank manager. When he was a child, Bakhtin developed a bone disease. His leg was amputated when he was thirty-seven. It is thought that his theorization about the grotesque and carnival is also partly due to his own experience of being an amputee. Starting in 1914, when Bakhtin was nineteen, he formed a group of intellectuals known as the "Bakhtin circle" who discussed social, cultural and religious issues posed by the Russian Revolution. Bakhtin was influenced by Søren Kierkegaard, the Christian philosopher, and attended meetings of the Voskresenie, a left-leaning political group that supported the Bolshevik's economic policy but resisted their commitment to atheism. In 1928, Bakhtin and members of the Bakhtin circle were arrested by the Soviet secret police for association with the Voskresenie, and he was charged with "philosophical idealism" and illicit religious activity. Bakhtin was sentenced to five years' work in a labor camp in Siberia, but because of his leg he was later commuted to exile to Kazakhstan with a prohibition against living in any major city. Like Freire, Bakhtin was a political exile.

While in exile, Bakhtin taught pedagogy in various places. He defended his doctoral thesis in 1946, but the affair was a scandal, in which his committee strongly defended him but the external reviewers would not accept his work. The government intervened and he was not awarded the doctoral degree. In 1967 his first arrest was annulled, and he was officially "rehabilitated" and was granted the freedom to live legally in Moscow, where he died in 1975.[2]

Bakhtin and Freire shared similar intellectual interests and had some biographical parallels. Both were political exiles, both were teachers, both elaborated their ideas of dialogue, "and both insisted on the situated socio-political nature"[3] of people and the word. Bakhtin writes specifically about language and how the subject and the other are constituted through dialogue.

Bakhtin and sociocultural theorist Lev Vygotsky[4] were of the same generation of the soviet intelligentsia. Although there is little evidence that Bakhtin and Vygotsky knew one another or influenced one another's work[5], the trajectories of their works from Russia into education internationally followed similar timelines. Now, Vygotsky and Bakhtin are often brought together in educational scholarship. Freire mentioned Vygotsky as an important influence[6], and it may be that within the nexus of these three scholars that there is room for fruitful elaborations of the socially mediated nature of learning and being. Bakhtin's major works include *Toward a Philosophy of the Act*, *Problems of Dostoevsky's Poetics*, *Rabelais and His World*, *The Dialogic Imagination*, and *Speech Genres and Other Late Essays*. Many of Bakhtin's writings were not well preserved and exist only as fragments. His writings were only translated into English beginning in the 1960s and his influence on education in the English-speaking world began only in the late 1980s.

Some of the most influential concepts to come out of Bakhtin's work are developed from his analysis of Dostoevsky's writings. In this analysis, Bakhtin interrogates how Dostoevsky's characters act and interact in the world, and he uses this analysis to comment on our humanity and the nature of our relationship to ourselves and one another.

Carnival

Bakhtin elaborates the carnival as a literary genre which allows for a different temporality and a different sense of human relations. A "carnival sense of the world" is one in which there is a "joyful relativity" which "weaken[s the world's] one-sided rhetorical seriousness, its rationality, its singular meaning, its dogmatism."[7] The carnival sense of the world is characterized by "a mighty life-creating and transforming power, an indestructible vitality."[8]

Bakhtin writes about carnival in a way that gives a sense of how he thinks about dialogue. Bakhtin traces the movement of literature from a consideration of an epic story—legends and myths that are very much tied to the tragic or comical past, to the genre of carnival. Bakhtin describes carnival as being about the now. Carnival is "on the plane of the present day, in a zone of immediate and even crudely familiar contact." Carnival "consciously rel[ies] on experience and on free invention." In this way, carnival can be critical or even a "cynical expose." Carnival resists a particular "stylistic unity" and is instead a "multi-styled and hetero-voiced nature of all these genres" with "multi-toned narration, the mixing of high and low, serious and comic." In this description of carnival, we see the germination of his thoughts about dialogue and what he calls "double voice-edness." Bakhtin says that in carnival, "[a]longside the representing word there appears the represented word; in certain genres a leading role is played by the double-voiced word. And what appears here, as a result, is a radically new relationship to the word as the material of literature." He then distinguishes between a Socratic form of dialogue in which Socrates' students dialogue in a process of coming to know the fixed and apparent irrefutable truth, and the kind of dialogue that emerges out of the genre of carnival:

> In carnival everyone is an active participant, everyone communes in the carnival act. Carnival is not contemplated and, strictly speaking, not even performed; its participants

live in it, they live by its laws as long as those laws are in effect; that is, they live a carnivalistic life.

Bakhtin draws a connection between carnival and the genre of satire that developed in response to Socrates, called "menippea" which Bakhtin suggests has the characteristic of carnival. Menippea allows for a "experimental fantasticality" and "extraordinary philosophical universalism and a capacity to contemplate the world on the broadest possible scale." Bakhtin writes,

> the organic combination within it of the free fantastic, the symbolic, at times even a mystical-religious element with an extreme and (from our point of view) crude slum naturalism. The adventures of truth on earth take place on the high road, in brothels, in the dens of thieves, in taverns, marketplaces, prisons, in the erotic orgies of secret cults, and so forth. The idea here fears no slum, is not afraid of any of life's filth. The man of the idea-the wise man-collides with worldly evil, depravity, baseness, and vulgarity in their most extreme expression. This slum naturalism is apparently already present in the earliest menippea.

Carnival is an interesting concept in relation to Freire, perhaps because Freire deals minimally with the creative and artistic aspects of the dialogic, preferring to discuss the political and pedagogical. However, there are clearly notes of harmonization here, with Bakhtin's invitation to dialogue as a creative process. There can also be a fruitful consideration of the varying uses of temporality in Bakhtin and Freire's writings. For example, Freire expresses a commitment to historically informed interpretations of present conditions, while also resisting the acceleration of our sense of time by contemporary media. Because Freire's writing is eminently concerned with the existent reality and the political nature of being, and perhaps also because of the Hegelian roots of his theorization of oppression, Freire's treats the good and evil as at odds with each other.

Freire writes,

> While *Homo sapiens* were emerging from the basic life-support structure, intervening creatively in the world, they invented language to be able to give a name to things that resulted from its intervention, "grasping" intellectuality and being able to communicate what had been "grasped." It was becoming simultaneously clear that human existence is, in fact, a radical and profound tension between good and evil, between dignity and indignity, between decency and indecency, between the beauty and the ugliness of the world. In other words, it was becoming clear that it is impossible to humanly exist without assuming the right and the duty to opt, to decide, to struggle, to be political.[9]

We see here a distinction between Bakhtin's carnival, which brings together wisdom and depravity in the setting of the slum, and Freire's notion of the "profound tension" between dignity and indignity. While Bakhtin uses the slum as a backdrop for a literary exploration of the variety of human experiences, Freire understands that the slum is a site for the reproduction of political domination.

Dialogue

Bakhtin ties self-consciousness and dialogue through an analysis of how the characters in Dostoyevsky talk to one another. Bakhtin develops an idea of self-consciousness in which the consciousness is not a priori to the dialogue. Rather, self-consciousness develops through a process of dialogue with another person. Bakhtin says that outside of this "living addressivity" self-consciousness does not exist. This can also be tied very closely to the way in which Freire thinks that dialogue can foster conscientization. However, for Freire, conscientization is a process of humanization (i.e., becoming fully human as a political animal), while for Bakhtin, he means a consciousness of one's own existence. There is a shared sense here of the relationship between dialogue and the realization of one's own subjectivity.

According to Bakhtin, "Only in communion, in the interaction of one person with another" can we know ourselves and one another. This dialogue is an end in itself, not the means to action. It is in dialogue that the person "becomes for the first time what he is." For Bakhtin, the important part of this is that dialogue creates not only the Self for the Other but the Self for the Self as well.

This comes close to Freire's statement in *Pedagogy of Freedom*: "Thinking correctly is, in other words, not an isolated act or something to draw near in isolation but an act of communication."

On dialogue, Freire says:

Critical and liberating dialogue, which presupposes action, must be carried on with the oppressed at whatever the stage of their struggle for liberation. The content of that dialogue can and should vary in accordance with historical conditions and the level at which the oppressed perceive reality. But to substitute monologue, slogans, and communiques for dialogue is to attempt to liberate the oppressed with the instruments of domestication. Attempting to liberate the oppressed without their reflective participation in the act of liberation is to treat them as objects which must be saved from a burning building; it is to lead them into the populist pitfall and transform them into masses which can be manipulated.

Bakhtin writes: "When dialogue ends, everything ends." If we think about this statement in terms of Freire's thinking about the pedagogical relationship between the teacher and the student, banking education can be understood as a lack of dialogue. The student in banking education does not, and is not allowed to, enter into a dialogue with a teacher, thus denying humanization and prohibiting the student to enter into the world via the educational structures. Freire says that the student brings their own experiences into the classroom. Reading Freire with Bakhtin, we would say that dialogue constitutes the creation of the student as self in relation to the teacher. If the teachers' speech consists of cultural invasion, and if the student is silenced, or forced to reproduce the dominant values of the teacher, the Self which will emerge in that interaction is Self as dominated object, rather than Self as creative Subject. Likewise, Bakhtin's sense that "[w]hen dialogue ends, everything ends" can also be read in terms of Freire's culture of silence among the peasants and of silencing the peasants.

In elaborating his ideas of dialogue, Bakhtin, like Freire, leaves room for conflicts, compliance, contradictions and rejoinders. We may say two things which are made to cohere even in their contradictions. People are complicated, capable of mockery and conviction, and the path from desire to deed may evade us, even in the process by which we convince ourselves of commitments through dialogue. Bakhtin explores in depth the limits, possibilities, and impossibilities for us to speak frankly to ourselves, to liberate ourselves, and to bring ourselves reconciliation. He sees that there are things we hide from one another, and things which we hide from ourselves, which can be revealed in the speech of others. He uses the concept of double-voicedness to explore how we verbalize both internal and external voices.

Unfinalized

Because Bakhtin chooses a literary critique of Dostoevsky, he was able to take his analysis into a discussion of the necessity of plot and the relation between dialogue and plot. One of his key ideas is that there is no resolution, conclusion, or solution— *"that internally unfinalizable something in man"*—which can never be understood in the monologic but only demonstrated in dialogue as an ongoing cycle. He explains this *unfinishedness*, as Freire would term it, with the concept of a *rejoinder.*

> Every thought of Dostoevsky's heroes (the Underground Man, Raskolnikov, Ivan, and others) senses itself to be from the very beginning a *rejoinder* in an unfinalized dialogue. Such thought is not impelled toward a well-rounded, finalized, systemically monologic whole. It lives a tense life on the borders of someone else's thought, someone else's consciousness.[10]

For Bakhtin, this unfinishedness goes into eternity, and here we see Bakhtin's religious sensibility.

For Freire, unfinishedness is an essential aspect of the possibility for hope. Unfinishedness is what allows us to perceive history as possibility. Awareness of one's own and the world's incompleteness is crucial to the process of conscientization and transformation. Freire discussed unfinishedness in relation to the purpose of education:

> Problem-posing education affirms men and women as beings in the process *of becoming*—as unfinished, uncompleted beings in and with a likewise unfinished reality. Indeed, in contrast to other animals who are unfinished, but not historical, people know themselves to be unfinished; they are aware of their incompletion. In this incompletion and this awareness lie the very roots of education as an exclusively human manifestation. The unfinished character of human beings and the transformational character of reality necessitate that education be an ongoing activity.[11]

Contrasting Dialectics and Dialogue

Bakhtin distinguishes between dialogue and the dialectic. For Bakhtin, the word "dialectic" has a pejorative of overtone.[12]

Bakhtin wrote in 1970, "Dialogue and dialectics. Take a dialogue and remove the voices . . . remove the intonations . . . carve out abstract concepts and judgments from living words and responses, cram everything into one abstract consciousness—and that's how you get dialectics."

Bakhtin understood the "dialectic" as the creation of abstract opposites. He gives the example of the two statements, "life is good" and "life is not good." Bakhtin says that these two utterances are judgments that be viewed as thesis and antithesis, then articulated together as a statement in a dialectical way in synthesis. But that, he says, is not dialogue. Dialogue is when judgments are embodied and given voice. In that embodied articulation of judgments, it is possible for these statements, utterances such as "life is good" and "life is not good," to come into dialogue with one another. For Bakhtin the distinction between dialogue and dialectic is that dialectic is an abstraction where dialogue is embodied. Bakhtin's dialogue does not require synthesis, rather, dialogue is "passing of a theme through many and various voices."

However, for Freire the dialectic is the fundamental nature of reality, as the relationship between subjectivity and objectivity: "[n]either objectivism nor subjectivism, nor yet psychologism is propounded here, but rather subjectivity and objectivity in constant dialectical relationship." Freire draws from the Hegelian master–slave dialectics the notion that the oppressed are characterized by their subordination to the consciousness of the master. "Then, true solidarity with the oppressed means fighting at their side to transform the objective reality which has made them these beings for another."[13] Part of the process of conscientization is to be able to understand the dialectical nature of reality. The oppressed "exist[s] in dialectical relationship to the oppressor, as his antithesis."

Freire understands the dialectic in terms of subjectivity and objectivity, not in terms of the abstract and the embodied. Freire explains subjectivity and objectivity in terms of the universal human experience of the dialectic contradiction of knowing oneself as object of history while at the same time being a subject of history.[14] When subjectivity and objectivity join, they produce a *dialectical unity* and that is how knowledge can be produced in solidarity with others through action. The oppressor can be in solidarity with the oppressed only when he no longer regards the oppressed as an abstract category. When the oppressor acknowledges the oppressed as persons who have been unjustly dealt with, silenced and deprived of their voices, deceived in their laboring and when the oppressor risks an act of love, only then can unity and solidarity be produced.[15] The task of the oppressed is to struggle for their liberation together with those who show true solidarity, and this acquires a critical awareness of oppression through the praxis of this struggle.[16] The process of knowing presumes a dialectical situation; "we think" constitutes "I think."[17] The dialectical unity, from which emerges knowledge, is closely linked with action.[18] Freire therefore understands dialectics in terms of praxis. "Human agency makes sense and flourishes only when subjectivity is understood in its dialectical, contradictory, dynamic relationship with objectivity, from which it derives."[19]

Freire was interested in structural relationships: the roles of the teacher and student in social production and reproduction. For Freire, critical literacy is an act of knowing.[20] Bakhtin is more interested in the psyche: the lies and promises we make to ourselves and one another and in micro-relationships and how we navigate being in the world through language. Freire describes a world that can be read, as it is, if we would only see it. He sees that people can become submerged in a silence—that is, an illiteracy—that makes the world illegible and takes social reality as given, determined, and pre-established, rather than as process in making.[21] Becoming aware of the world's unfinishedness requires reading the word and the world. For Freire, literacy is therefore key, and the elimination of illiteracy among the popular classes is key in Freirean educational praxis. Reading the word and reading the world become a metaphor for living itself, and life in this sense means a political life. For Bakhtin, talking is the same thing as consciousness, that is living at all.

CHAPTER 9

Freire and Foucault

Paul-Michel Foucault was a French philosopher and psychologist. He was born on October 15, 1926, in France—the middle child of Anne Malapurt and her husband Paul Foucault. Although his given name was Paul, after his father, Anne called him "Michel," and this is the name Foucault himself preferred and by which his work is widely known. Foucault was gay; living under the legal and cultural repression of homosexuality in Europe in the twentieth century shaped his life and informed his perspectives and the themes in his writing. Foucault suffered from depression. He attempted suicide at age twenty-two and was taken to see a psychologist who diagnosed his depression as related to keeping his sexuality a secret. The experience of psychotherapeutic treatment piqued his interest in psychiatry, and he earned degrees in both philosophy and psychology.[1]

Foucault lived for a period in exile in Sweden, where he sought to escape from the sexual restrictions he experienced in France. This period of exile contributed to his personal reflection on his own life and how he, as a gay man, should fight daily repression and disciplinary techniques. During that time, in the 1950s in Sweden, Foucault matriculated into the University of Uppsala and attempted to earn his doctoral degree. His thesis was rejected by Sten Lindroth, a historian with a positivistic orientation who thought that Foucault's writing was overwrought and poorly done.[2]

Perhaps more than other writers in this book, Foucault was deliberate in communicating that his works were an expression of the struggles within his own life.[3] In the end, Foucault was a prodigious writer, and many of his works have been translated from French to English. He has had an enormous impact on a wide range of areas, such as history, psychology, law, criminology, education, healthcare, sexuality, and gender studies. Foucault gives his theoretical starting points from an ontological perspective about the nature of society and social relations, what he has called "the history of systems of thought." Foucault's work also provides several different methodological contributions, for example the genealogical method and Foucauldian discourse analysis. I begin with a consideration of Foucault's contribution with a brief introduction of these two methods so that we may consider what Foucault means by discourse and the relationship between Freire's dialogue and Foucault's discourse. Beginning with method, or the analytical tools Foucault uses to understand the world, gives us a window into how he comes to his conclusions regarding the possibilities for liberation and agency.

Dialogue and Discourse

Foucault uses the term "discourse" to refer to systems of knowledge production: the way we talk about and understand the world. Because the power to control the way we talk about the world also means control of the way we think about and perceive who we are and what the world is, Foucault was very interested in the control of discourse and how this control constitutes complex and productive power relations in society. This is a post-structuralist perspective. We approach the topic of knowledge not from discovering a universal truth but from the perspective of how truth is constructed, how knowledge is represented, and who determines this knowledge production. Foucault sees that discourse is not only constructing knowledge but also constructing and limiting the possibilities for our own subjectivities—that is, who we can be in the world.

From the methodological perspective of the Foucauldian discourse analysis, we ask how we can look at what Foucault calls "signs" (e.g., language, text, art, and architecture) and how these signs articulate with one another in ways that are patterned. These patterns determine the sort of rules that govern the representation and relationship between objects and subjects. By analyzing these representations, we can uncover how power operates. Foucault's genealogical method drew on the work of Nietzsche to develop a method of analyzing history, with the aim of tracing the historical development of things "we tend to feel are without history,"[4] that is the fundamental institutions in modern society such as prisons, hospitals, and schools, and how these institutions have come into being.

Foucault's first book, *Madness and Civilization*, was published in 1961, when he was thirty-six. The book traces how the idea of madness has been understood in Europe over time, using a method that deconstructs and critiques how madness has been defined. Here we may also find a resonant chord with Freire, in that Foucault critiqued the modern common sense that everything is better now than it was previously in history. Foucault rejects the notion that human beings are now more humane and that the institutions of modern society are more humane than their precursors. In *Disciple and Punish*, which is about the birth of the prison, Foucault makes the argument that even though in the past punishment was public and very violent, the systems we have now are no less violent. They have simply moved punishment behind closed doors in a way that makes punishment seem as if it were free of violence; it sanitizes and normalizes violence.

Foucault's genealogical method tries to uncover the inconsistencies in history, not understanding history as a coherent linear progression but uncovering contradictions and inconsistencies. The method seeks to identify origin points of where certain ideas emerged, and how and where they came to be accepted, and to what extent, in what circles of people have accepted them. The genealogical method starts with the fact that some concept or practice has come to be accepted and works to trace backward the "system of acceptability" what system of knowledge and power (i.e., what *discourse*) supports the legitimacy of, for example, the idea of madness, the prison, the techniques of the prison, or the techniques of the military. In this analysis, Foucault is working with the body. Whereas Freire is interested in our conceptualization of the world and in humanization through dialogue between the teacher and student, Foucault's theory and analysis rely heavily on the body as the site of the inscription of power.

Freire understood dialogue as a practice—a practice by which we achieve liberation. It is an enactment in the world, a connection between theory and materiality in action. If we blend here Freire and Foucault, discourse could be understood as the content of a dialogue. It is the normative means of social control. That is, how control is accomplished in the ways that we discipline our bodies to act in certain socially acceptable ways. However, Foucault and Freire think differently about the agent, about where power resides, about where it is contested, and about what empowerment can mean. One area where these differing understandings come to bear is in notions of knowledge and awareness of one's own political subjectivity, or political self. Foucault was interested in the relationship between knowledge production and power; he was interested in knowledge itself and the ways that knowledge is historically constructed and historically contingent. His work concerned the ways that we internalize and reproduce our consent through our bodies and language. In this way, Foucault is not working with class struggle but understands power as something which is much more diffuse and is reproduced in a myriad of minuscule ways through techniques that have no definite center. There is therefore a difference between how Foucault thought about power and social relations, and the tradition that informs Freire. Freire's work is largely informed by the Frankfurt school. He employed a Hegelian oppositional and binary framing of oppressor and oppressed, which he uses to discuss the dialectical relation between the two in order to understand histories of oppression and domination. Freire sees this relation as contextual and that all people can exist as both oppressor and oppressed. Because of this, Freire is able to develop his radical democratic humanism[5] as a dialogical and pedagogical response to oppression, which operates between people and is founded on an ontological commitment to humanization. Foucault is coming from a different line of Marxist tradition, having studied under the French Marxist philosopher Althusser. Althusser and Foucault, in structuralist and post-structuralist tradition, decline humanism and make a more structurally deterministic approach, which emphasizes the complex ways that power works and is structurally reproduced to determine economic, political, cultural, and ideological possibilities for being.

Foucault traces this connection between the production of knowledge and power as a study of history, and some of his most notable works include *Madness and Civilization*, *The Birth of the Clinic*, and *Discipline and Punish*. In *Discipline and Punish* he analyzes the historical development of the modern penal systems and the move from execution to incarceration and total control of criminals. Foucault demonstrates the ways in which strict discipline and morals have transformed the agency of punishment from the corporeal to the spiritual. In the idea of docility, that is the collective coercion of bodies, Foucault sees that we discipline ourselves from an internal state. Foucault calls this discipline "techniques of the self." Discipline is not only from the external threat of bodily punishment. Foucault critiques this "military dream of society" as being a kind of utopia of docile bodies. He extends this analysis into schools and "the means of correct training." This line of thought opens up ideas about surveillance and supervision. Foucault sees that in schools, as well as other institutions, surveillance is everywhere, always, as a permanent, continuous field. At the same time, this surveillance is "discreet" and accomplished in silence. Surveillance is one of many concepts in Foucault's work that are useful for theorizing space and power.

Power and Truth

Foucault thinks power is everywhere and can be understood as a "regime of truth." He recognizes that power is not only negative, coercive, or repressive—it is also productive. Power *produces* something in society. What power produces is our reality, it produces our "rituals of truth." We see here that Foucault connects power with truth as a social production.

> Truth is a thing of this world: it is produced only by virtue of multiple forms of constraint. And it induces regular effects of power. Each society has its regime of truth, its "general politics" of truth: that is, the types of discourse which it accepts and makes function as true; the mechanisms and instances which enable one to distinguish true and false statements, the means by which each is sanctioned; the techniques and procedures accorded value in the acquisition of truth; the status of those who are charged with saying what counts as true.[6]

Foucault critiques modes of inquiry that attempt to take on the status of science through a process of objectification. For example, economies and wealth production are analyzed through the measurement and examination and objectification of the productive subject. Human existence is objectified in the study of natural history. Modes of objectifying work through "dividing practices," whether that be dividing the subject from others or dividing the subject internally. Such divisions create clear and clean separations between the good and bad, the sick and healthy, and the rich and poor.

Biopower and Biopolitics

Foucault's concept of biopower is "[a] power that exerts a positive influence on life, that endeavours to administer, optimize, and multiply it, subjecting it to precise controls and comprehensive regulations." Biopolitics is a political rationality that aims "to ensure, sustain, and multiply life, to put this life in order." For Foucault, biopower is productive. It *does something* in society, but it does so with coercion, seduction, manipulation, and violence. Schooling is one such method of control, and Foucault argues that "[c]ontrol is inscribed in the architecture" of schools. This brings an important connection to Freire's critique of banking education, as well as Freire's critique of neoliberal capitalism. Foucault connects biopower and capitalism, saying "[t]his bio-power was without question an indispensable element in the development of capitalism" which made possible "the controlled insertion of bodies into the machinery of production and the adjustment of the phenomena of population to economic processes." Foucault's work on biopower has been expanded later in the writings of Achille Mbembe, who has used Foucault's concept of biopolitics, which refers to the control of life, to talk about *necropolitics*, which is the control of death, who dies and the control of Black bodies.[7] Mbembe elaborates this concept with historical and contemporary analyses of the state's right to kill, using the example of colonialism and the Nazi regime.

Subjectification

Freire and Foucault share a consideration of the processes by which people are rendered as subjects or objects in society. The process of subjectification is becoming a subject, and this also means the subjugation of certain discourses related to ways of knowing and being. Foucault writes, "My objective . . . has been to create a history of the different modes by which, in our culture, human beings are made subjects. My work has dealt with three modes of objectification which transform human beings into subjects."[8] The first mode of objectification is "objectivizing of the productive subject, the subject who labors," the second mode of objectification is when "the subject is either divided inside himself or divided from others," and finally "the way a human being turns himself into a subject." Although Freire's work can also be considered from the perspective of each of these three objectifications, it is perhaps most clear to see how Freire addressed the second mode, in terms of the objectification that occurs when people become divided into oppressors and oppressed, and the historical and situational contextualization of this process.

Comparisons between Foucault and Freire

One of Foucault's great contributions is his consideration of the specific methods, or techniques, that are used to produce power and the overlap between the material, corporeal, social, and psychological exercises of power. It's interesting to relate this back to Freire because Freire discusses pedagogy and in some way, pedagogy can include techniques and methods, for example methods of teaching literacy. These methods can be oppressive or can be liberatory, for example banking education can be understood as an oppressive technique. In comparison to Freire, Foucault is more interested in the body and the control of space. Freire, on the other hand, is more interested in our inner and political life. For Freire, liberation requires the liberation of the consciousness—yet conscientization is necessary but not sufficient for liberation. A clear distinction between Freire and Foucault is the extent to which they think liberation is possible. They see differently the role of the social and collective in the process of liberation—if liberation is even possible. For Foucault, social relations of mutual recognition can hold dangerous illusions and function as masked tools for subordination, while for Freire mutual recognition and dialogue hold crucial importance in liberation.

Foucault can offer us some questions for reflection on Freire's work. For example, what are the mechanisms of oppression for Freire? If we use Foucault's language to reflect on Freire, how is pedagogy distinct from method? There could also be possibilities, from a Freirean perspective, to open up Foucault's ontological assumptions and what could be meant by Freire's *dehumanization* in a Foucauldian reading. Freire can also pose the question to Foucault: how can people, who are constantly within the process of subjection, find ways of making clear the ethical-political perspectives that inform the critique of the historical present? In other words, on what grounds can a critique or resistance be advocated or justified by Foucault? How can people collectively formulate objectives and common goals about what to resist? It is in response to these questions that Freire takes us into the realm of hope through radical humanism, while Foucault rather leaves us in the blinding light of an oppressive ideological structure we can barely resist, let alone change.

CHAPTER 10

Freire and Bourdieu

Noëmie Duhau gave birth to Pierre Felix on August 1, 1930, in the small village of Denguin in southern France. Noëmie had married Albert Bourdieu against the wishes of her parents, who came from a line of landowners and regarded Albert as a person of lesser social status, coming from the peasantry. Bourdieu's parents were supportive of his education, and Albert instilled in Pierre a concern for the destitute: "He taught me without speaking, and above all with his attitude, to respect 'the lesser,' among whom he counted himself, and also even if he never explicitly said it, their struggles."[1] Bourdieu did well in school and eventually studied philosophy alongside the French philosopher Louis Althusser in Paris. He worked as a teacher for one year before he was conscripted in 1955 into the French Army and sent to Algeria. His first book, *Sociologie de L'Algérie* published in French in 1958 and translated into English in 1962 as *The Algerians* cemented his position as a sociologist.[2]

Bourdieu wrote extensively about the reproduction of power, especially in educational settings. Like Freire, Bourdieu also writes from a Marxist tradition, although one informed by Althusser. Bourdieu takes the notion of *capital* as a foundational structure in modern societies which forms social and power relations. He elaborates the concept of capital along three axes: social, cultural, and economic. Freire and Bourdieu share this reinterpretation of Marx and also a concern for how education functions to reproduce the structures of society.

Social Capital

Bourdieu's theory of the different forms of capital explains the different ways of converting power in a capitalist society. Bourdieu writes,

> Capital can present itself in three fundamental guises: as economic capital, which is immediately and directly convertible into money and may be institutionalized in the form of property rights; as cultural capital, which is convertible, in certain conditions, into economic capital and may be institutionalized in the form of educational qualifications; and as social capital, made up of social obligations ("connections"), which is convertible, in certain conditions, into economic capital and may be institutionalized in the form of a title of nobility.[3]

Both Bourdieu and Freire write about the specific ways education works to reproduce capital. Bourdieu wrote about how society, through the family and the educational systems, generates academic capital, while also limiting who can access it. "Academic capital is in fact the guaranteed product of the combined effects of cultural transmission by the family and cultural transmission by the school (the efficiency of which depends on the amount of cultural capital directly inherited from the family)."[4]

Freire's notions of capital are not developed to the same extent in his writing, but he does describe the function of education in a capitalist society.

> In a capitalist society, the education of workers has as one of its goals the continuation of a class of wage earners, obliged to sell their labor to the capitalist class. The

education required to continue reproducing this class is one that will continuously increase the efficiency of the workers in their participation in the work process. This process, as Marx points out, is one involving "objects bought by the capitalist, objects that belong to him": labor, on the one hand; the means of production on the other.[5]

Symbolic Violence

When Bourdieu talks about the "symbolic" he is talking primarily about language: "linguistic relations are always relations of symbolic power."[6] Bourdieu writes, "All pedagogic action (PA) is, objectively, symbolic violence insofar as it is the imposition of a cultural arbitrary by an arbitrary power."[7] Bourdieu relates symbolic violence to Marx, saying, "[Symbolic violence] is a similar concept to the Marxist idea of 'false consciousness,' whereby people internalise the discourses of the dominant, meaning that 'the most intolerable conditions of existence can so often be perceived as acceptable and even natural.'"[8]

Any symbolic domination presupposes on the part of those who are subjected to it a form of complicity which is neither a passive submission to an external constraint nor a free adherence to values. . . . The specificity of symbolic violence resides precisely in the fact that it requires of the person who undergoes it an attitude which defies the ordinary alternative between freedom and constraint.[9]

Doxa

Bourdieu connects symbolic violence to his idea of *doxa*, or the unquestioned truths of a society.

Furthermore, having accepted as legitimate the established (inequitable) social order and their position within it, individuals who are powerless and dominated believe the doxa which attributes blame to themselves for their subordinate position.

Doxa refers to the learned, fundamental, deep-founded, unconscious beliefs, and values, taken as self-evident universals, that inform an agent's actions and thoughts within a particular field. Doxa tends to favor the particular social arrangement of the field, thus privileging the dominant and taking their position of dominance as self-evident and universally favorable. Therefore, the categories of understanding and perception that constitute a habitus, being congruous with the objective organization of the field, tend to reproduce the very structures of the field. A doxic situation may be thought of as a situation characterized by a harmony between the objective, external structures and the "subjective," internal structures of the habitus. In the doxic state, the social world is perceived as natural, taken-for-granted and even commonsensical.

Critical Approaches of Freire and Bourdieu

Bourdieu introduced a wide range of concepts that produce a critical reading of social relations and the role of education in society. His concepts of habitus, the learned sociocultural ways of being, and cultural reproduction, the process by which culture is reproduced, find points of articulation with Freire's understanding of how education socializes people into the cultural values of the oppressor. However, there are several points of divergence between Bourdieu and Freire, beginning with their understandings of agency and resistance. Bourdieu understands subversive action as such:

The specific efficacy of subversive action consists in the power to bring to consciousness, and so modify, the categories of thought which help to orient individual and collective practices and in particular the categories through which distributions are perceived and appreciated.[10]

Perhaps the greatest synergy between the two writers can be found in Bourdieu's writings about the colonial situation in Algeria, in which he describes the situation of the domination of the traditional Algerian culture.

Moreover, the whole of this society was being torn asunder by the hidden or open tensions that existed between the dominant European society and the dominated Algerian society. Now the evolution of the colonial system causes the gap (and the correlative tension) which separates the dominant and the dominated societies to keep on widening, and this occurs in all the spheres of existence—economic, social and psychological. The almost stationary state of equilibrium in which the colonial society was maintained is the resultant of two opposing forces whose strength. The Algerians is constantly increasing: on the one hand, the force that tends to bring about an increase in inequalities and in real discrimination, a consequence due in part to the pauperization of the people and to the disintegration of the original Algerian culture; on the other hand, the force constituted by the feelings of revolt and resentment aroused against this increase in social inequalities and discrimination. In short, when carried along by its own internal logic, the colonial system tends to develop all the consequences implied at the time of its founding—the complete separation of the social castes. Violent revolution and repression by force fit in perfectly with the logical coherence of the system; while the colonial society is as unintegrated as ever, the war now became completely integrated within the colonial system and allowed it to be recognized for what it really is. Indeed, the war plainly revealed the true basis for the colonial order: the relation, backed by force, which allows the dominant caste to keep the dominated caste in a position of inferiority.[11]

CHAPTER 11

Freire and Young

Iris Marion Young was born on January 2, 1949, in New York City. She completed her doctorate in philosophy in 1974 from Pennsylvania State University, becoming a political philosopher and feminist scholar. Her work, often responding to Sartre, de Bouivour, Heidegger, and Habermas and engaging extensively with the work of contemporary feminist philosophers, explores the gendered nature of society and themes of justice and democracy. Young's perspectives on women's roles in the family and society were greatly impacted by her own experience as a child. She wrote of her childhood:

[It was] a perfect picture of '50s family bliss, with one flaw: my mother didn't clean the house. Our two-bedroom apartment was always dirty, cluttered, things all over the floors ... My mother spent her days at home reading books, taking a correspondence course in Russian ... But she also played with us—authors, rummy, twenty-questions, with gusto-and sang and sag, teaching us hymns and old army songs ... Then my daddy died—quickly, quietly, of a brain tumor. My mother was devastated ... My mother drank, but never on Sunday morning. My sister and I went to school sad, my brother stayed home with our mother, who had less motive than ever to clean the house. We were not poor ... just messy. But one spring day a uniformed man came into my class and called my name. He escorted me to a police car where my brother and sister were already waiting. Without explanation, they drove us to a teen-reform home . . . Slowly I learned or inferred that she had been thrown in jail for child neglect.[1]

Young reflected on the social circumstances of her childhood,

A woman alone with her children in this development of perfectly new squeaky clean suburban houses. She is traumatized by grief, and the neighbors look from behind their shutters, people talk about the disheveled way she arrives at church, her eyes red from crying. Do they help this family, needy not for food or clothes, but for support in a very hard time? A woman with her children is no longer a whole family, deserving like others a respectful distance . . . A woman alone with her children is liable to punishment, including the worst of all for her: having her children taken from her. Neglect. The primary evidence of neglect was drinking and a messy house . . . We were a family in need of support, but we children were not neglected.[2]

Young became professor of political science at the University of Chicago. She died in 2006 at age fifty-seven of esophageal cancer. Young is remembered for her gentle humor and optimism.

Young was very much concerned with the concept of justice, which she argued should be approached not from the perspective of an ideal sense of justice but rather from a practical analysis of the forms which oppression takes in society. In doing this, she outlines the "five faces of oppression."

Oppression

Young offers a rich definition of oppression, expanding the ways that domination manifests, particularly in relation to "decision making, division of labor, and culture."[3]

Oppression consists in systematic institutional processes which prevent some people from learning and using satisfying and expansive skills in socially recognized settings, or institutionalized social processes which inhibit people's ability to play and communicate with others or to express their feelings and perspective on social life in contexts where others can listen.[4]

Young does not see oppression as an individual phenomenon but as something that "happens to social groups."[5] She then "suggest[s] that oppression names in fact a family of concepts and conditions" which she "divide[s] into five categories: exploitation, marginalization, powerlessness, cultural imperialism, and violence."[6] *Exploitation* is the "steady process of the transfer of the results of the labor of one social group to benefit another."[7] *Marginalization* occurs to people whom "the system of labor cannot or will not use." Young elaborates:

Marginalization is perhaps the most dangerous form of oppression. A whole category of people is expelled from useful participation in social life and thus potentially subjected to severe material deprivation and even extermination.

Powerlessness is experienced by "those over whom power is exercised without their exercising it; the powerless are situated so that they must take orders and rarely have the right to give them." Moreover,

Powerlessness also designates a position in the division of labor and the concomitant social position that allows persons little opportunity to develop and exercise skills. The powerless have little or no work autonomy, exercise little creativity or judgment in their work, have no technical expertise or authority, express themselves awkwardly, especially in public or bureaucratic settings, and do not command respect.[8]

The fourth category, *cultural imperialism*, evokes Freire's *cultural invasion*, which Freire defines as such:

> [C]ultural invasion, which like divisive tactics and manipulation also serves the ends of conquest. In this phenomenon, the invaders penetrate the cultural context of another group, in disrespect of the latters potentialities; they impose their own view of the world upon those they invade and inhibit the creativity of the invaded by curbing their expression.

> Whether urbane or harsh, cultural invasion is thus always an act of violence against the persons of the invaded culture, who lose their originality or face the threat of losing it. In cultural invasion (as in all the modalities of antidialogical action) the invaders are the authors of, and actors in, the process; those they invade are the objects. The invaders mold; those they invade are molded. The invaders choose; those they invade follow that choice—or are expected to follow it. The invaders act; those they invade have only the illusion of acting, through the action of the invaders.[9]

Young describes cultural imperialism in similar terms:

> Those living under cultural imperialism find themselves defined from the outside, positioned, placed, by a network of dominant meanings they experience as arising from elsewhere, from those with whom they do not identify and who do not identify with them. Consequently, the dominant culture's stereotyped and inferiorized images of the group must be internalized by group members at least to the extent that they are forced to react to behavior of others influenced by those images. This creates for the culturally oppressed the experience that W.E.B. Du Bois called "double consciousness"—"this sense of always looking at one's self through the eyes of others, of measuring one's soul by the tape of a world that looks on in amused contempt and

pity."[10] Double consciousness arises when the oppressed subject refuses to coincide with these devalued, objectified, stereotyped visions of herself or himself. While the subject desires recognition as human, capable of activity, full of hope and possibility, she receives from the dominant culture only the judgment that she is different, marked, or inferior.[11]

Systematic *violence* is the final expression of oppression described by Young:

> Members of some groups live with the knowledge that they must fear random, unprovoked attacks on their persons or property, which have no motive but to damage, humiliate, or destroy the person. In American society women, Blacks, Asians, Arabs, gay men, and lesbians live under such threats of violence, and in at least some regions Jews, Puerto Ricans, Chicanos, and other Spanish-speaking Americans must fear such violence as well. Physical violence against these groups is shockingly frequent.[12]

Social Justice

Young's conception of justice, and specifically of social justice, derives from her description of oppression. "The concepts of domination and oppression, rather than the concept of distribution, should be the starting point for a conception of social justice."[13] Young therefore "define[s] social justice then as the institutional conditions for promoting self-development and self-determination of a society's members."[14]

Young and Freire: The Geographies of Justice

Young's treatment of oppression is a clear point of synergy with Freire. But her work, in addition to exploring women's rights, democracy, and difference, touches on a very interesting notion of the spatiality of justice, which could also be considered in Freire's work. Young was enchanted with the political and demographic possibilities of the city, specifically with the possibility for difference.[15] For Young, cities are places of "unassimilated otherness and difference." Her own childhood experience of the white cookie-cutter suburbs of New Jersey where her mother was harshly scrutinized and her eventual move with her mother back to "the safe indifference of New York City" informed her notions of the spatiality of power as realized in social relations.

As an aesthetic, the ideal notion of the city is interesting because Freire worked with peasants in rural areas. The geographies of oppression are not unimportant to Freire's work, but he approaches the question of the relation between place and liberation not only in relation to the land but in relation to the significance of land *ownership*. Freire sees this connection as fundamentally individualistic: "It is not to become free that [the peasants] want agrarian reform, but in order to acquire land and thus become landowners—or, more precisely, bosses over other workers."

CHAPTER 12

Unfinished Conversations

Critical theory is a dialogue. Gramsci's work is a commentary, exploration, and critique of Marx. Gramsci thought Marx missed or misunderstood the relationship between culture and power. Fromm thought Marx missed the psychological side of alienation. hooks thought Freire's work was androcentric and missed a gendered, intersectional understanding of oppression and the possibilities for liberation. Bakhtin disagreed with Marx's secular ideals. Fraser expanded on Habermas, filling what she saw as the gaps in his understanding of how the public sphere is mediated by the power dynamics of misrecognition. Freire asks us what liberation can mean in education.

Throughout this book there runs a critique of Marx in the form of various elaborations and contestations of how power is produced. Against a simplistic or monolithic reading of critical theory, these various twentieth-century scholars engage with the insights and blind spots of Marx and one another, through a nuanced and sincere engagement with questions of domination, history, and materiality. There also runs throughout the book a continual nod to Hegel, which emerges as a defense of the need to read Hegel, so as to position the philosophical heritage to which contemporary social theory, particularly critical theory, responds.

Dialogue takes time. It should not be thought of in a naïve way, as if talking itself would lead to resolution. Rather, dialogue means seeing others as partners worthy of learning with and learning from. Nor should dialogue be understood in a mechanistic way, where the speech act itself represents dialogue. Dialogue, in this way, represents a labor, a curiosity that extends beyond the interaction. Contemporary critical scholars such as Vanessa Andreotti have described this in terms of *gesturing toward*. Thinking of dialogue in terms of gesture and bodily movement suggests that what is accomplished through dialogue is also accomplished by laboring together, which at times requires waiting patiently for organic processes to proceed according to their own gentle time. For those with a pedagogical orientation, this is critical. Sometimes, it is hard to talk. It can be hard to think of something to say, to express an assurance or an uncertainty. But we can work together with our bodies. We labor together, side-by-side, and this is solidarity. Not simply an ideological affinity or affirmation but solidarity with others in action.

As you and I are not together in body, I leave you with this request from myself to you, dear reader, in Paulo Freire's words:

> I will be satisfied if among the readers of this work there are those sufficiently critical to correct mistakes and misunderstandings, to deepen affirmations and to point out aspects I have not perceived.

NOTES

Preface

1 Italo Calvino, *Italo Calvino: Letters, 1941–1985* (Princeton: Princeton University Press, 2013), p. 454.

2 Raymond Morrow Allen and Carlos Alberto Torres, "Re-Reading Freire and Habermas: Philosophical Anthropology and Reframing Educational Research in the Neoliberal Anthropocene," in *The Wiley Paulo Freire Handbook*, edited by C. A. Torres (Malden, MA and Oxford: WileyBlackwell, 2019), 241–74.

3 Martin Carnoy, *Foreword to Paulo Freire: Pedagogy of the Hearth* (London: Bloomsbury, 2021).

4 Martin Carnoy and Rebeca Tarlau, "Paulo Freire Continued Relevance for U.S. Education," in *The Wiley Handbook of Paulo Freire*, edited by Carlos Alberto Torres (Hoboken, NJ: Wiley/Blackwell, 2019), 221–37.

5 What are the most cited publications in the social sciences (May 12, 2016) https://blogs.lse.ac.uk/impactofsocialsciences/2016/05/12/what-are-the-most-cited-publications-in-the-social-sciences-according-to-google-scholar/.

6 P. Mayo, "Synthesizing Gramsci and Freire: Possibilities for a Theory of Radical Adult Education," *International Journal of Lifelong Education* 13, no. 2 (1994): 125–48.

7 Raymond Allen Morrow and Carlos Alberto Torres, *Reading Freire and Habermas. Critical Pedagogy and Transformative Social Change* (New York: Teachers College, Columbia University, 2002).

8   P. O'Cadiz, P. Linquist Wong, and C. A. Torres, *Democracy and Education. Paulo Freire, Educational Reform and Social Movements in Brazil* (Boulder, CO: Westview Press, 1998).

Introduction

1   Paulo Freire, *Letters to Cristina*, trans. D. Macedo (New York and London: Routledge, 1996), 13.

2   Donaldo Macedo, "Foreword," in *Pedagogy of Freedom: Ethics, Democracy, and Civic Courage*, Paulo Freire (Lanham, MD: Rowman & Littlefield Publishers, 1998), xiv.

3   Harvard Graduate School of Education, *Pedagogy of the Oppressed: Noam Chomsky, Howard Gardner, and Bruno della Chiesa Askwith Forum*. YouTube, May 24, 2013. https://youtu .be/2Ll6M0cXV54.

4   Antonia Darder, *Reinventing Paulo Freire: A Pedagogy of Love* (London: Routledge, 1997).

5   Carlos Alberto Torres, *Education, Power, and Personal Biography: Dialogues with Critical Educators* (New York: Routledge, 1997), 1.

6   Zvi Eisikovits and Chaya Koren, "Approaches to and Outcomes of Dyadic Interview Analysis," *Qualitative Health Research* 20, no. 12 (2010): 1642–55.

7   Paulo Freire, *Pedagogy of the Oppressed* (New York: Bloomsbury, 2018).

8   Ibid.

9   See the works by Torres and Morrow, including Carlos Alberto Torres and Raymond Allen Morrow, "Paulo Freire, Jürgen Habermas, and Critical Pedagogy: Implications for Comparative Education," *Critical Studies in Education* 39, no. 2 (1998): 1–20; Raymond Allen Morrow and Carlos Alberto Torres, *Reading Freire and Habermas: Critical Pedagogy and Transformative Social Change* (New York: Teachers College Press, 2002); and Raymond Allen Morrow and Carlos Alberto Torres, "Rereading Freire and Habermas: Philosophical Anthropology and Reframing Critical Pedagogy and Educational Research in the Neoliberal Anthropocene," in *The Wiley Handbook of Paulo Freire*, ed. Carlos Alberto Torres (New York: Wiley-Blackwell, 2019), 239–74.

Chapter 1

1 Erich Fromm, *The Revolution of Hope, Toward a humanized Technology*, Vol. 38 (New York: Harper & Row, 1968), 121.

2 The Centro Intercultural de Documentación (Center for International Documentation) was a school for training development workers and Catholic missionaries founded by Roman Catholic priest Ivan Illich and colleagues in 1965. The aim was to train local clergy, in response to the Papal command to send US and Canadian priests to Latin America. Illich's most well-known book on education, *Deschooling Society* (1972), grew out of his seminars at the Center.

3 See Rainer Funk, *Erich Fromm: His Life and Ideas, An Illustrated Biography* (New York: A&C Black, 2000), 138 and Robert Lake and Vicki Dagostino, "Converging Self/Other Awareness: Erich Fromm and Paulo Freire on Transcending the Fear of Freedom," in *Paulo Freire's Intellectual Roots: Towards Historicity in Praxis*, ed. Robert Lake and Tricia Kres (New York: Bloomsbury, 2013), 101–26.

4 Erich Fromm, *Escape from Freedom* (New York: Macmillan, 1994).

5 Ibid., 3.

6 Erich Fromm, "The Application of Humanist Psychoanalysis to Marx's Theory," *Socialist Humanism: An International Symposium*, ed. Erich Fromm (New York: Doubleday, 1965), 207–22.

7 Paulo Freire, *Pedagogy of the Oppressed* (New York: Continuum International Publishing Group Ltd., 2005), 77.

8 Ibid., 68.

9 Ibid., 47.

10 Fromm, *Escape from Freedom*, 36–7.

11 Erich Fromm, *The Art of Loving: The Centennial Edition* (New York: A&C Black, 2000).

12 Freire, *Oppressed*, 3.

13 Erich Fromm, *The Sane Society* (United States: Open Road Media, 2013), 233.

14 Erich Fromm, *Man for Himself: An Inquiry into the Psychology of Ethics* (London: Routledge, 1947).

15 Freire, *Oppressed*, 152.

16 Ibid., 45.
17 Ibid., 48.
18 Erich Fromm, *The Heart of Man: Its Genius for Good and Evil* (Riverdale, NY: American Mental Health Foundation Books, 2010), 128.
19 I would like to thank Frederica Raia for her insights into Fromm's description of agency and the Other.

Chapter 2

1 bell hooks, "bell hooks Speaking about Paulo Freire—The Man, His Work," in *Paulo Freire: A Critical Encounter*, ed. Peter Leonard and Peter McLaren (London: Routledge, 2002), 151.
2 Ibid.
3 Following Kimberlé Crenshaw, Neil Gotanda, and many other critical race scholars, Black, Indigenous, and Color are capitalized, while white and western are written in lowercase. White is capitalized at the beginning of a sentence or when capitalized by the original author. This choice is an effort to avoid the affirmation of white power, racial domination, and Western cultural hegemony (see also K. W. Crenshaw, "Toward a Race-Conscious Pedagogy in Legal Education," *National Black Law Journal* 11 (1988): 1–14, R. Drake and A. Oglesby, "Humanity Is Not a Thing: Disrupting White Supremacy in K-12 Social Emotional Learning," *Journal of Critical Thought and Praxis* 10, no. 1 (2020): 1–22, N. Gotanda, "A Critique of Our Constitution Is Color-Blind," *Stanford Law Review* 44 (1991): 1, R. Kohli, *Teachers of Color: Resisting Racism and Reclaiming Education* (Cambridge, MA: Harvard Education Press, 2021).; R. Kohli and M. Pizarro, "The Layered Toll of Racism in Teacher Education on Teacher Educators of Color," *AERA Open* 8 (2022): 23328584221078538., L. Pérez Huber and D. G. Solorzano, "Racial Microaggressions as a Tool for Critical Race Research," *Race Ethnicity and Education* 18, no. 3 (2015): 297–320.)
4 bell hooks, *Keeping a Hold on Life: Reading Toni Morrison's Fiction* (Santa Cruz: University of California, Santa Cruz, 1983), 65–6.

5 bell hooks, "Theory as Liberatory Practice," *Yale JL & Feminism* 4 (1991): 2.

6 bell hooks, *Teaching to Transgress* (London: Routledge, 2014), 148.

7 bell hooks, *Teaching Critical Thinking* (London: Routledge, 2010), 20.

8 Ibid., 31.

9 hooks, *Teaching to Transgress,* 148.

10 Paulo Freire, *Pedagogy of the Oppressed* (New York: Continuum International Publishing Group Ltd., 2005), 84.

11 hooks, *Teaching to Transgress,* 11.

12 bell hooks, *All About Love: New Visions* (New York: Harper Perenial, 2001), 76.

13 bell hooks, *Salvation: Black people and love* (New York: Harper Perennial, 2001), 112.

14 Ibid., 225.

15 Paulo Freire, *Pedagogy of Freedom: Ethics, Democracy, and Civic Courage* (Oxford: Rowman & Littlefield Publishers, 1998), 45.

16 bell hooks, *Killing Rage: Ending Racism* (New York: Henry Holt & Company, 1995), 16.

17 Freire, *Freedom.*

18 Ibid., 11.

19 bell hooks, *Teaching Community: A Pedagogy of Hope* (New York: Routledge, 2003).

Chapter 3

1 Enrique Dussel, *The Pedagogics of Liberation: A Latin American Philosophy of Education* (New York: Punctum Books, 2019), 155.

2 Ibid., 165.

3 Freire, *Pedagogy of the Oppressed,* 154.

4 Dussel, *The Pedagogics of Liberation,* 166.

5 Ibid., 170.

6 Enrique Dussel, Javier Krauel, and Virginia C. Tuma, "Europe, Modernity, and Eurocentrism," *Nepantla: Views from South* 1, no. 3 (2000): 474.

Chapter 4

1 Lewis R. Gordon, *What Fanon Said: A Philosophical Introduction to His Life and Thought* (New York: Fordham University Press, 2015), 26.
2 The National Liberation Front in Algeria, or *Front de libération nationale* (FLN), unified the nationalist movement against French colonial rule in the Algerian war of independence from 1954 to 1962.
3 Frantz Fanon, *The Wretched of the Earth*, trans. R. Philcox (New York: Grove Press, 1961).
4 Frantz Fanon, *Black Skin, White Masks* (New York: Grove Press, 2008).
5 Fanon, *The Wretched of the Earth*, 53.
6 Ibid., 11.
7 Ibid., 68.
8 Ibid., 135.
9 Paulo Freire, *Education for Critical Consciousness* (New York: Bloomsbury, 2013), 17.

Chapter 5

1 Andrew Pearmain, *Antonio Gramsci: A Biography* (New York: Bloomsbury, 2020).
2 Ibid.
3 Raymond Allen Morrow and Carlos Alberto Torres, *Social Theory and Education: A Critique of Theories of Social and Cultural Reproduction* (New York: SUNY Press, 1995).
4 A. Gramsci, *Selections from the Prison Notebooks*, ed. and trans. Q. Hoare and G. Nowell-Smith (London: Lawrence & Wishart, 1971), 331.
5 Ibid., 698.
6 Ibid., 747.
7 Freire, *Pedagogy of the Oppressed* 51.
8 Ibid., 51–2.
9 Gramsci, *Selections from the Prison Notebooks*, 248.
10 Freire, *Pedagogy of the Oppressed*, 141.
11 Gramsci, *Selections from the Prison Notebooks*, 135.

12 Ibid., 137.
13 Ibid., 138.
14 Ibid., 143.
15 Paulo Freire, *Pedagogy in Process Letters from Guinea-Bisseau* (New York: Bloomsbury, 2021), 104.
16 Peter Mayo, *Antonio Gramsci and Educational Thought* (Oxford: Wiley-Blackwell, 2010), 1.
17 This connection to adult education is elaborated by Peter Mayo.
18 Peter Mayo, *Gramsci, Freire and Adult Education: Possibilities for Transformative Action* (London: Zed Books, 1999).

Chapter 6

1 Kenneth Baynes, *Habermas* (New York: Routledge, 2015).
2 Jürgen Habermas, *Between Naturalism and Religion: Philosophical Essays* (Cambridge: Polity, 2008).
3 Baynes, *Habermas,* 10.
4 Freire, *Pedagogy of the Oppressed*, 135–6.
5 Raymond Allen Morrow and Carlos Alberto Torres, *Reading Freire and Habermas: Critical Pedagogy and Transformative Social Change* (New York: Teachers College Press, 2002).
6 Raymond Allen Morrow and Carlos Alberto Torres, "Re-Reading Freire and Habermas: Philosophical Anthropology and Reframing Educational Research in the Neoliberal Anthropocene," in *The Wiley Paulo Freire Handbook*, ed. Carlos Alberto Torres (Malden, MA and Oxford: Wiley-Blackwell, 2019), 241–74.
7 Samantha Ashenden, "On Violence in Habermas's Philosophy of Language," *European Journal of Political Theory* 13, no. 4 (2014): 427–52.

Chapter 7

1 Laura Lee Downs and Jacqueline Laufer, "Nancy Fraser, Rebel Philosopher," *Travail, Genre et Societes* 27, no. 1 (2012): 5–27.
2 Hanne Marlene Dahl, Pauline Stoltz, and Rasmus Willig, "Recognition, Redistribution and Representation in Capitalist

Global Society: An Interview with Nancy Fraser," *Acta Sociologica* 47, no. 4 (2004): 380.

3 Hegelian Marxism refers to the use of Hegel's philosophy to interpret Marxist theory.

4 Nancy Fraser, "Heterosexism, Misrecognition, and Capitalism: A Response to Judith Butler," *Social Text* 52/53 (1997): 280.

5 Freire, *Pedagogy of the Oppressed*, 36.

6 Ibid., 90.

7 Nancy Fraser, "Feminist Politics in the Age of Recognition: A Two-Dimensional Approach to Gender Justice," *Studies in Social Justice* 1, no. 1 (2007): 27.

8 Ibid., 28.

9 Ibid., 29.

10 Freire, *Oppressed*.

11 Nancy Fraser and Nancy A. Naples, "To Interpret the World and to Change It: An Interview with Nancy Fraser," *Signs: Journal of Women in Culture and Society* 29, no. 4 (2004): 1103–24.

12 Dahl, Stoltz and Willig, "Recognition, Redistribution and Representation in Capitalist Global Society," 380.

Chapter 8

1 Thomas Seifrid, "Mikhail Bakhtin's Heritage in Literature, Arts, and Psychology. Art and Answerability," Ed. by Slav N. Gratchev and Howard Mancing. Lanham, NY: Lexington Books, 2018.

2 Caryl Emerson, "Mikhail Bakhtin," in *Filosofia: An Encyclopedia of Russian Thought*, ed. Alyssa DeBlasio and Mikhail Epstein (2019); available online: https://filosofia .dickinson.edu/encyclopedia/bakhtin-mikhail/.

3 Peter Rule, "Bakhtin and Freire: Dialogue, Dialectic and Boundary Learning," *Educational Philosophy and Theory* 43, no. 9 (2011): 924–42.

4 Lev Vygotsky was a Soviet psychologist whose work on the social determinants of human development became a basis for sociocultural theory in education, including the notion of the zone of proximal development.

5 Caryl Emerson. "The outer Word and Inner Speech: Bakhtin, Vygotsky, and the Internalization of Language," *Critical Inquiry* 10, no. 2 (1983): 245–64.

6 Peter Mayo, *Antonio Gramsci and Educational Thought* (Oxford: Wiley-Blackwell, 2010), 8.

7 Mikhail Bakhtin, *Problems of Dostoevsky's Poetics*, vol. 8 (Minnesota: University of Minnesota Press, 2013), 107.

8 Ibid.

9 Paulo Freire, *Pedagogy of Freedom: Ethics, Democracy and Civic Courage* (New York: Rowman & Littlefield Publishers, 2000), 53.

10 Ibid., 32.

11 Freire, *Pedagogy of the Oppressed*, 84.

12 Emerson, "Mikhail Bakhtin."

13 Freire, *Pedagogy of the Oppressed*, 31.

14 Paulo Freire, "Pedagogy of Indignation, Paradigm Publishers," *London* 120 (2004): 15–16.

15 Freire, *Pedagogy of the Oppressed*, 31–2.

16 Ibid., 33.

17 Paulo Freire, *The Politics of Education: Culture, Power, and Liberation* (London: Greenwood Publishing Group, 1985), 99–100.

18 Freire, *Pedagogy of the Oppressed*, 38.

19 P. Freire and D. Macedo, *Literacy: Reading the Word and the World* (London: Routledge, 1987), 59.

20 Paulo Freire, "The Adult Literacy Process as Cultural Action for Freedom," *Harvard Educational Review* 40, no. 2 (1970): 205–25.

21 Freire, *The Politics of Education*, 103.

Chapter 9

1 David Macey, *The Lives of Michel Foucault* (Brooklyn, NY: Verso Books, 2019), 36.

2 Ibid., 80.

3 Ibid., x–xi.

4 Michel Foucault, "Nietzsche, Genealogy, History," in *Language, Counter-Memory, and Practice: Selected Essays and Interviews*, ed. Donald F. Bouchard (Ithaca, NY: Cornell University Press, 1977), 139.

5   See the works of Stanley Aronowitz, including *Roll over Beethoven: The Return of Cultural Strife* (Hanover, New Hampshire: Wesleyan University Press, 1993) and *Against Schooling: For an Education that Matters* (London: Routledge, 2015).

6   Paul Rabinow, *The Foucault Reader* (London: Penguin, 1991).

7   Achille Mbembe, "Necropolitics," in *Foucault in an Age of Terror: Essays on Biopolitics and the Defence of Society*, ed. Stephen Morton and Stephen Bygrave (London: Palgrave Macmillan, 2008), 152–82.

8   Michel Foucault, "The Subject and Power," *Critical Inquiry* 8, no. 4 (1982): 777–95.

Chapter 10

1   Terry Rey, *Bourdieu on Religion: Imposing Faith and Legitimacy* (London: Routledge, 2014).

2   Michael James Grenfell, *Pierre Bourdieu* (New York: Bloomsbury Publishing, 2014).

3   Pierre Bourdieu, "The Forms of Capital. (1986)," *Cultural Theory: An Anthology* 1 (2011): 81–93.

4   Pierre Bourdieu, *Distinction: A Social Critique of the Judgment of Taste* (Cambridge, MA: Harvard University Press, 1979), 23.

5   Paulo Freire, *Letters to Cristina*, trans. D. Macedo (New York and London: Routledge, 1996), 108–9.

6   Loic J. Wacquant and Pierre Bourdieu, *An Invitation to Reflexive Sociology* (Cambridge: Polity, 1992), 1–59.

7   Pierre Bourdieu and Jean-Claude Passeron, *Reproduction in Education, Society and Culture* (London: Sage, 1977), 5.

8   Mustafa Emirbayer and Victoria Johnson, "Bourdieu and Organizational Analysis," *Theory and Society* 37 no. 1 (2008): 46.

9   Pierre Bourdieu, "Les rites comme actes d'institution," *Actes de la recherche en sciences sociales* 43 no. 1 (1982): 36.

10 Pierre Bourdieu, *The Logic of Practice* (Stanford, CA: Stanford University Press, 1990), 141.

11 Bourdieu, *Algerians* (Boston, MA: Beacon Press, 1962), 145–6.

Chapter 11

1 Iris Marion Young, *Intersecting Voices: Dilemmas of Gender, Political Philosophy, and Policy* (Princeton, NJ: Princeton University Press, 1997).

2 Meena Dhanda, "Theorising with a Practical Intent: Gender, Political Philosophy and Communication. An Interview with Iris Marion Young," *Women & Philosophy Review* 26 (2000): 1–22.

3 Iris Marion Young, *Justice & the Politics of Difference* (Princeton, NJ: Princeton University Press, 2011), 33.

4 Ibid., 38.

5 Ibid., 9.

6 Ibid., 40.

7 Ibid., 49.

8 Ibid., 57.

9 Freire, *Pedagogy of the Oppressed*, 152.

10 W. E. B. Du Bois, *The Souls of Black Folk: Essays and Sketches* (Greenwich, CT: Fawcett, 1961), 45.

11 Young, *Justice & the Politics of Difference*, 59–60.

12 Ibid., 61.

13 Ibid., 62.

14 Iris Marion Young, *Inclusion and Democracy* (Oxford: Oxford University press on demand, 2002), 33.

15 Iris Marion Young, "The Ideal of Community and the Politics of Difference," *Social Theory and Practice* 12, no. 1 (1986): 1–26.

REFERENCES

Aronowitz, S. (1993), *Roll over Beethoven: The Return of Cultural Strife*, Hanover, New Hampshire: Wesleyan University Press.

Aronowitz, S. (2015), *Against Schooling: For an Education that Matters*, New York: Routledge.

Ashenden, S. (2014), "On Violence in Habermas's Philosophy of Language," *European Journal of Political Theory*, 13 (4): 427–52.

Bakhtin, M. (2013), *Problems of Dostoevsky's Poetics*, Minnesota: University of Minnesota Press.

Baynes, K. (2015), *Habermas*, New York: Routledge.

Bourdieu, P. (1962), *The Algerians*, Boston: Beacon Press.

Bourdieu, P. (1979), *Distinction: A Social Critique of the Judgment of Taste*, Cambridge, MA: Harvard University Press.

Bourdieu, P. (1982), "Les rites comme actes d'institution," *Actes de la recherche en sciences sociales*, 43 (1): 58–63.

Bourdieu, P. (1990), *The Logic of Practice*, Stanford, CA: Stanford University Press.

Bourdieu, P. (2011), "The Forms of Capital.(1986)," *Cultural Theory: An Anthology*, 1: 81–93.

Bourdieu, P. and J.-C. Passeron (1977), *Reproduction in Education, Society and Culture*, London: Sage.

Crenshaw, K. W. (1988), "Toward a Race-Conscious Pedagogy in Legal Education," *National Black Law Journal*, 11: 1–14.

Dahl, H. M., P. Stoltz, and R. Willig (2004), "Recognition, Redistribution and Representation in Capitalist Global Society: An Interview with Nancy Fraser," *Acta Sociologica*, 47 (4): 374–82.

Darder, A. (2017), *Reinventing Paulo Freire: A Pedagogy of Love*, New York: Routledge.

Dhanda, M. (2000), "Theorising with a Practical Intent: Gender, Political Philosophy and Communication. An Interview with Iris Marion Young," *Women & Philosophy Review*, 26: 1–22.

Downs, L. L. and J. Laufer (2012), "Nancy Fraser, Rebel Philosopher," *Travail, Genre et Societes*, 27 (1): 5–27.

Drake, R. and A. Oglesby (2020), "Humanity is Not a Thing: Disrupting White Supremacy in K-12 Social Emotional Learning," *Journal of Critical Thought and Praxis*, 10 (1): 1–22.

Du Bois, W. E. ([1903] 1961), *The Souls of Black Folk: Essays and Sketches*, Greenwich, CT: Fawcett.

Dussel, E. D. (2019), *The Pedagogics of Liberation: A Latin American Philosophy of Education*, New York: Punctum Books.

Dussel, E. D., J. Krauel, and V. C. Tuma (2000), "Europe, Modernity, and eurocentrism," *Nepantla: Views from South*, 1 (3): 465–78.

Eisikovits, Z. and C. Koren (2010), "Approaches to and Outcomes of Dyadic Interview Analysis," *Qualitative Health Research*, 20 (12): 1642–55.

Emerson, C. (1983), "The Outer Word and Inner Speech: Bakhtin, Vygotsky, and the Internalization of Language," *Critical Inquiry*, 10 (2): 245–64.

Emerson, C. (2019), "Mikhail Bakhtin," in A. DeBlasio and M. Epstein (eds.), *Filosofia: An Encyclopedia of Russian Thought*. Available online: https://filosofia.dickinson.edu/encyclopedia/bakhtin-mikhail/.

Emirbayer, M. and V. Johnson (2008), "Bourdieu and Organizational Analysis," *Theory and Society*, 37 (1): 1–44.

Fanon, F. (2004), *The Wretched of the Earth,* trans. R. Philcox. New York: Grove Press.

Fanon, F. (2008), *Black Skin, White Masks*, New York: Grove Press.

Fraser, N. (2007), "Feminist Politics in the Age of Recognition: A Two-Dimensional Approach to Gender Justice," *Studies in Social Justice*, 1 (1): 23–35.

Fraser, N. and N. A. Naples (2004), "To Interpret the World and to Change it: An Interview with Nancy Fraser," *Signs: Journal of Women in Culture and Society*, 29 (4): 1103–24.

Freire, P. (1970), "The Adult Literacy Process as Cultural Action for Freedom," *Harvard Educational Review*, 40 (2): 205–25.

Freire, P. (1996), *Letters to Cristina,* trans. D. Macedo, New York and London: Routledge.

Freire, P. (1998), *Politics and Education*, Los Angeles: UCLA Latin American Center Publications.

Freire, P. (1998), *Pedagogy of Freedom: Ethics, Democracy and Civic Courage*, New York: Rowan & Littlefield Publishers.

Freire, P. (2004), *Pedagogy of Indignation*, London: Paradigm Publishers.

Freire, P. (2005), *Pedagogy of the Oppressed, 30th Anniversary Edition*, trans. M. Bergman Ramos, intr. D. Macedo, New York: Continuum International.

Freire, P. (2014), *Pedagogy of Solidarity*, Walnut Creek: Left Coast Press, Inc.

Freire, P. (2018), *Pedagogy of the Oppressed*, New York: Bloomsbury.

Freire, P. (2021), *Pedagogy of the Heart*, New York: Bloomsbury.

Freire, P. (2021), *Pedagogy of Hope: Reliving Pedagogy of the Oppressed*, New York: Bloomsbury.

Freire, P. (2021), *Pedagogy in Process: The Letters to Guinea-Bissau*, New York: Bloomsbury.

Freire, P. and D. Macedo (1987), *Literacy: Reading the Word and the World*, London: Routledge.

Fromm, E. (1941), *Escape from Freedom*, New York: Rinehart.

Fromm, E. (1947), *Man for Himself: An Inquiry into the Psychology of Ethics*, London: Routledge.

Fromm, E. (1965), "The Application of Humanist Psychoanalysis to Marx's Theory," in E. Fromm (ed.), *Socialist Humanism: An International Symposium*, 207–22. Doubleday.

Fromm, E. (1968), *The Revolution of Hope, Toward a Humanized Technology*, Vol. 38, New York: Harper & Row.

Fromm, E. (1994), *Escape from Freedom*, New York: Macmillan.

Fromm, E. (2000), *The Art of Loving: The Centennial Edition*, New York: Continuum Publishing Group Inc.

Fromm, E. (2010), *The Heart of Man: Its Genius for Good and Evil*, Riverdale, NY: American Mental Health Foundation Books.

Fromm, E. (2013), *The Sane Society*, New York: Open Road Media.

Funk, R. (2000), *Erich Fromm: His Life and Ideas, An Illustrated Biography*, New York: Continuum Publishing Group Inc.

Gordon, L. R. (2015), *What Fanon Said: A Philosophical Introduction to his Life and thought*, New York: Fordham University Press.

Gotanda, N. (1991), "A Critique of our Constitution is Color-Blind," *Stanford Law Review*, 44: 1.

Gramsci, A. (1971), *Selections from the Prison Notebooks*, ed. and trans Q. Hoare and G. Nowell-Smith, London: Lawrence & Wishart.

Gratchev, S. and H. Mancing (2018), *Mikhail Bakhtin's Heritage in Literature, Arts, and Psychology. Art and Answerability*, Lanham, MD: Lexington Books.

Grenfell, M. J. (2014), *Pierre Bourdieu*, New York: Bloomsbury.

Harvard Graduate School of Education. (2013), *Pedagogy of the Oppressed: Noam Chomsky, Howard Gardner, and Bruno della Chiesa Askwith Forum*. May 24. Available Online: https://youtu .be/2Ll6M0cXV54.

hooks, b. (1983), *Keeping a Hold on Life: Reading Toni Morrison's Fiction*, Santa Cruz: University of California, Santa Cruz.

hooks, b. (1991), "Theory as Liberatory Practice," *Yale JL & Feminism*, 4: 1–12.

hooks, b. (1995), *Killing Rage*, New York: Routledge.

hooks, b. (2001), *All about Love: New Visions*, New York: Harper Perennial.

hooks, b. (2001), *Salvation: Black People and Love*, New York: Harper Perennial.

hooks, b. (2010), *Teaching Critical Thinking: Practical Wisdom*, New York: Routledge.

hooks, b. (2014), *Teaching to Transgress*, New York: Routledge

Kohli, R. (2021), *Teachers of Color: Resisting Racism and Reclaiming Education*, Cambridge, MA: Harvard Education Press.

Kohli, R. and M. Pizarro (2022), "The Layered Toll of Racism in Teacher Education on Teacher Educators of Color," *AERA Open*, 8: 23328584221078538.

Lake, R. and V. Dagostino (2013), "Converging Self/Other Awareness: Erich Fromm and Paulo Freire on Transcending the Fear of Freedom," in R. Lake and T. Kres (eds.), *Paulo Freire's Intellectual Roots: Towards Historicity in Praxis*, 101–26, New York: Bloomsbury.

Macedo, D. (1998), "Foreword," in P. Freire (ed.), *Pedagogy of Freedom: Ethics, Democracy, and Civic Courage*. Lanham, MD: Rowman & Littlefield Publishers.

Mayo, P. (1999), *Gramsci, Freire and Adult Education: Possibilities for Transformative Action*. London: Zed Books.

Mayo, P. (2010), *Antonio Gramsci and Educational Thought*, 1. Oxford: Wiley-Blackwell.

Mbembe, A. (2008), "Necropolitics," in Stephen Morton and Stephen Bygrave (eds.), *Foucault in an Age of Terror*. London: Palgrave Macmillan.

Morrow, R. A. and C. A. Torres (2002), *Reading Freire and Habermas: Critical Pedagogy and Transformative Social Change*, New York: Teachers College Press.

Morrow, R. A. and C. A. Torres (2019), "Rereading Freire and Habermas: Philosophical Anthropology and Reframing Critical Pedagogy and Educational Research in the Neoliberal Anthropocene," in C. A. Torres (ed.), *The Wiley Handbook of Paulo Freire*, 239–74, Hoboken, NJ: Wiley-Blackwell.

Oksala, J. (2016), "Affective Labor and Feminist Politics," *Signs: Journal of Women in Culture and Society*, 41 (2): 281–303.

Pearmain, A. (2020), *Antonio Gramsci: A Biography*, New York: Bloomsbury.

Pérez Huber, L. and D. G. Solorzano (2015), "Racial Microaggressions as a Tool for Critical Race Research," *Race Ethnicity and Education*, 18 (3): 297–320.

Rabinow, P. (1991), *The Foucault Reader*, London: Penguin.

Rey, T. (2014), *Bourdieu on Religion: Imposing Faith and Legitimacy*, London: Routledge.

Rule, P. (2011), "Bakhtin and Freire: Dialogue, Dialectic and Boundary Learning," *Educational Philosophy and Theory*, 43 (9): 924–42.

Torres, C. A. (1997), *Education, Power, and Personal Biography: Dialogues with Critical Educators*, New York: Routledge.

Torres, C. A. and R. A. Morrow (1998), "Paulo Freire, Jürgen Habermas, and Critical Pedagogy: Implications for Comparative Education," *Critical Studies in Education*, 39 (2): 1–20.

Wacquant, L. J. and P. Bourdieu (1992), *An Invitation to Reflexive Sociology*, Cambridge: Polity.

Young, I. M. (1986), "The Ideal of Community and the Politics of Difference," *Social Theory and Practice*, 12 (1): 1–26.

Young, I. M. (1997), *Intersecting Voices: Dilemmas of Gender, Political Philosophy, and Policy*, Princeton, NJ: Princeton University Press.

Young, I. M. (2002), *Inclusion and Democracy*, Oxford: Oxford University Press on Demand.

Young, I. M. (2011), *Justice and the Politics of Difference*, Princeton, NJ: Princeton University Press.

INDEX

Page numbers followed with "n" refer to endnotes.